the new york book of golf

By Nick Nicholas

universe publishing

To my wife, Cristyne, our moms and dads, our families, and Gabby: Thank you for everything.

First published in the United States of America in 2004
by UNIVERSE PUBLISHING
A Division of Rizzoli International Publications, Inc.
300 Park Avenue South
New York, NY 10010
www.rizzoliusa.com

© 2004 by Nick Nicholas
Cover design by Paul Kepple and Jude Buffum @ Headcase Design
www.headcasedesign.com
Cover illustration by Mary Lynn Blasutta
Interior design by Headcase Design

2003 2004 2005 2006 2007 / 10 9 8 7 6 5 4 3 2 1

Distributed to the U.S. trade by St. Martin's Press, New York

Printed in the United States of America

ISBN: 0-7893-1055-4

Library of Congress Catalog Control Number: 2004103537

contents

foreword

by Bill Castner

When people find out that I am a PGA golf professional from New York City, they often comment, "You must be very good at playing off the cement."

It is true, that when one thinks about the virtues of the Big Apple, images of huge skyscrapers, wonderful bridges and landmarks, great eating establishments, spellbinding theater, interesting museums, exquisite art galleries, world-class shopping, and the best people-watching opportunities anywhere quickly come to mind.

But New York City has never been considered a golf destination. Yet, in every borough, there are incredible golf opportunities. New York City golfers are blessed with many inexpensive and eclectic golf opportunities; they just need to be committed and determined. It is definitely challenging and rewarding to be a golfer in New York City.

A golfer living in Manhattan has all of the resources necessary to become a great golfer but has to struggle to take advantage of them. To practice, he or she must fight gridlock to get to Chelsea Piers or pay a toll to get to Randalls Island Golf Center. Most players do not own a car and so must board a bus or train with clubs. This is always an interesting proposition. To play, you must leave the borough to take advantage of one of the public courses. Sometimes getting there is not half the fun.

To play at Van Cortlandt Park, the closest and easiest 18-hole golf course to get to from Manhattan, a golfer will enjoy a train ride on the 1 or 9 train, take a short stroll through the park, and arrive at the historic clubhouse at the lake that the Van Cortlandts created decades ago. Walking to the first tee, golfers will see the swans and ducks lounging on the lake. Starting out with a short par-4 with the woods lurking on the right and a tough small green, the round has only just begun.

In order to make this golf day happen, some planning is necessary. Reservations must be made. Waits at the tee and on the golf course may have to be tolerated. Four-hour rounds are rare. The golf course will be crowded and play will be slow (especially on weekends). You might be playing with a rank beginner or a hustler looking for a money game. Conditions will not be like those you see on tour telecasts. Etiquette is sometimes, at best, minimal. Remember, you are golfing in the Concrete Jungle.

Don't give up hope yet—there is a positive side. You will be treated to playing two 600-yard par-5s and several 200-yard par-3s. You will play a fun and interesting golf course that always provides a memorable day of fresh air and exercise. You will also meet many other very interesting New York golfers and will probably make some new friends. In the end, it will definitely be worth all the effort.

I grew up at Dyker Beach Golf Course, located in Brooklyn and shadowed by the Verrazano-Narrows Bridge. During the 1960s, Dyker Beach was known as the busiest golf course in the world. Every year more than 100,000 rounds were played at Dyker. My brother and I started caddying as young teenagers. Soon a golfer gave us clubs and we were playing almost every day.

The local golf professional, Tom Strafaci, took an interest in me and taught me about the golf swing. Tom, in many ways, was way ahead of his time. He was a great teacher, player, and supporter of junior golf. He always said, "There is no such thing as a bad kid on the golf course."

Thanks to Tom Strafaci, I became a golfer and have had the opportunity to serve professionally in every borough of New York City. I have been exposed to the wonderful layouts and the great people who frequent them. Tom was a legend and had a passion for New York City golf.

I believe that Nick Nicholas has that same passion. *The New York Book of Golf* is a greatly informative manual and will provide many hours of pleasure. If you aren't playing golf, what is better than reading about it? Use this guide to find out where to play and how to plan to play there. A worthwhile goal is to play at least one golf course in every borough and collect a scorecard from each place.

During the 1970s and 1980s the golf courses were poorly managed and became run-down. New York City was undergoing financial crises and the golf courses suffered. Golfers were forced to travel outside the city to play.

Recently, New York City golf courses have undergone a renaissance. Expert management companies and innovative mom-and-pop proprietors have been brought in to manage and maintain them. Mayors Rudolph Giuliani and Michael Bloomberg, both passionate golfers, have spearheaded many improvements at every golf course, along with the help of the New York City Parks Department. Irrigation, golf cart paths, new tee areas, and lakes have been installed. I understand more improvements are being planned for the future. These are your golf courses. Enjoy them.

introduction

Spend five minutes in Myrtle Beach, South Carolina, where I golfed and wrote about golf for years, and you too would be bitten by the golf bug. There, you'd swear each road leads to a golf course, a driving range, or a store filled with the latest golf equipment. The courses are beautiful, the weather is perfect, and most importantly, there are enough options to satisfy every golfer's wildest dreams.

But four years ago brought a change of U.S. Open proportions: I moved from the golf capital of the United States to the Big Apple. I'm an extremely lucky guy to have found the perfect lady—a New Yorker, of course. But marriage meant relocating.

It helps that my wife, Cristyne, gets just as excited as I do about trying to smack the white pellet down the fairway. I'll also note she hits it with a slight draw and uncanny consistency off the tee.

She warned me about the change of address, though.

Strike that. "Warned" is too negative. Let's simply say she prepared me.

Cristyne said I would never be able to simply leave our Manhattan apartment with clubs in tow, walk down Second Avenue, and yank the headcover off my driver and swing away.

Not only would the guy who runs the corner fruit stand nervously duck behind his produce, but I would also surely be ticketed by a couple of New York City's Finest for, let's say it in golf terms, hitting out of bounds. Their penalty is more costly than the United States Golf Association's two-stroke fine.

But not to worry, my wife informed me plenty of golf exists in and around Manhattan. You simply have to own the right map. New York features memorable destinations, such as the country's oldest public golf course, Van Cortlandt; the 2002 and 2009 U.S. Open site, Bethpage Black; and a driving range like no other, Chelsea Piers. Simply highlight the correct route, board a train or subway line, and you're on your way. So for the last four years I've been searching to get on course, so to speak, in the New York area.

And, where did the tracks take me?

While the quantity of golf compressed into Myrtle Beach isn't in the five boroughs, I've discovered that the quality of golf in the metropolitan area exceeds all expectations.

It may sound contradictory, but the city golfer must be aggressive and, at the same time, exhibit patience from the first tee to the 18th green.

Did someone mention patience? There's traffic. There are five-hour rounds. So relax. Enjoy your trip to the course. Enjoy the golf, the breeze at your back, the friendship of the foursome, and your best shot of the day.

getting on course

Golfing in New York takes a certain amount of determination. PGA teaching professional Bill Castner initially learned to play at popular Dyker Beach and later worked for a handful of the New York City courses. He says it takes bulletproof mettle for golfers to survive and enjoy New York City's busy municipal golf circuit.

Used as an intangible 15th club, the love of the game carries golfers onto subways, buses, trains, even ferries to and from Staten Island, and into taxis to their destinations. City players mix in with the rush-hour straphangers, their iron club heads noticeably clanking along the way

There are times when the wait and walk involved in hailing a cab can be frustratingly long. So agonizing is the wait that you're ready to place a golf ball on a curb, pull out a 3-iron, and smack a low liner off a yellow car door to get a cabbie's attention.

If it rains, pray you packed your rain suit and umbrella. Not just to use on the course, but also on the streets.

To a visitor, getting on course likely is an afterthought. Their routine may be as easy as calling for a tee time an hour before they play. Getting to the course is never an issue for them. So forgive them for not knowing any better. Your foursome can't be laid back and show up at noon without a tee time. You'll struggle to get in 18 or 9 holes or may be turned back altogether. Use the phone reservation system and call early and often. It will make getting on course an easier game.

Determination won't help you reach the green in two shots on the 620-yard second hole at Van Cortlandt or spin back an iron shot within gimme range on Kissena Park's signature ninth.

It will, however, get you through, around, and past 8 million residents to reach your favorite city course.

"Often you find that golfers who do play in New York City, they really love golf," says Tom Sutter, head professional at the Golf Club at Chelsea Piers. "They're willing to put up with the problems that exist financially and physically to play golf. They're not casual golfers. They don't do it because it's near their house, it's right across the street, or their friends are doing it because they want to have a beer after the round. That's not why they play golf.

"They play golf because they love to play golf. Their level of enthusiasm is great. As you live in the city you see that in a lot of activities, not only golf. They're very avid about it. You're not going to last with all the difficulties thrown in front of you, the roadblocks, unless you love it."

For the record, Queens has the most opportunities for play with five courses: Clearview, Douglaston, Forest Park, Kissena Park, and a private course, Towers Country Club.

The Bronx is unique in that it has the oldest public course in the country, Van Cortlandt, and the city's only 36-hole facility at Pelham Bay/Split Rock. Mosholu, a nine-hole course with an extensive practice area, is also in the Bronx.

By the summer of 2006, drivers on the Bronx Whitestone Bridge, will notice players finally swinging away on the Jack Nicklaus–designed Ferry Point Golf Course.

Staten Island is a hotbed of competitive players. They hone their talents at La Tourette, Silver Lake, and South Shore. It's also home to a private course, Richmond County Country Club.

And Brooklyn offers legendary Dyker Beach and Robert Trent Jones's Marine Park.

Manhattan? There really isn't a course, unless you count one of the two full-swing game simulators at Chelsea Piers or the only outdoor golf course in the 212 area code, the now-defunct par-3 layout on Governor's Island, a decommissioned Coast Guard base. Manhattan also chips in with an Off-Broadway play devoted to the little white ball. "Golf: The Musical" is a 90-minute parody about the sport, teeing off at the John Houseman Theater Center on West 42nd Street.

These courses are not perfect. When they generate 60,000; 70,000; or 80,000 rounds a year, it's physically impossible to keep them in the same shape as your country club's course that hosts only 20,000 rounds annually.

But city golfers should do their part to fix what's wrong, mainly by raking bunkers and repairing divots in the fairways and on the greens. My father always said to treat people like you'd want to be treated. I would never want to try and blast out from someone's footprint or be forced to sink a putt where players previously dragged their cleats.

The Top Ten Reasons to Love New York City Golf

1. Fine conditions. New York City courses are in their best shape because of recent irrigation overhauls.

2. VIP sightings. Maybe you'll play alongside stars of stage or screen or politicians or judges. Then again, maybe you'll have more fun exchanging stories with one or two of the city's average Joes.

3. Course characters. Nowhere is there a more helpful guide than a New York City course regular. Just don't give 'em any strokes.

4. Price is still right. Though raised in recent years, fees still beat the $150-plus green fee at your favorite resort or increased "non-resident" fees just outside the five boroughs.

5. The card. A $6 resident card allows city dwellers yearly use for reduced green fees. Cost is only $2 for seniors (62 and over) and juniors (17 and under).

Residents can purchase their card at any of the pro shops. Be prepared to have your picture taken.

6. Join the club. Some courses have men, women, and/or senior leagues with openings for those who want a little competition or companionship.

7. Just in time. With walk-up tee times, mainly for singles and twosomes, you can sometimes get on course without a long wait.

8. Double your pleasure. The two-course facility at Pelham Bay/Split Rock doubles your chance of getting a good tee time and makes it easier to play 36 in one day.

9. Closed? Almost never. Most courses are open 365 days a year. That is, unless snow blankets the fairways and greens.

10. No backyard "fore!" Unlike resort courses, city layouts are, for the most part, free of condos and houses bordering their courses.

suiting up

Major-league shopping and Manhattan continue their synonymous relationship. Name the product, and there is a 99.9 percent chance it's here. Somewhere.

Shopping for golf accessories can be as satisfying as getting on course. Remember purchasing that state-of-the-art, shiny, extra long, graphite-shafted. . .golf umbrella?

No?

Seriously, what about the new, titanium-faced driver that requires forking out nearly a week's pay? Confess that launching rapid-fire perfect connections into the store's full-sized net makes you feel like a scratch golfer. A moment after the cashier hands you the club, you can't wait to take it out on the course and show off your new precision and distance.

Golfers attack the retail game as a sport within the sport.

They're always in hot pursuit of discounts for their particular brand of golf balls on sale at X Store, Y Store, or Z Store. If X Store has a better price than Y and Z, you better believe word of the sale will travel fast. Soon, stores Y and Z will likely match the price.

The same can be said about clubs and shoes. But differences in prices, especially in new clubs, aren't significant. The key is to have patience and wait for prices to drop. That newfangled putter may be $200-something today. But, if possible, wait until supply greatly exceeds demand, and you'll be rewarded with a smarter purchase.

Most golfers can't wait, however. They want the latest gadget yesterday so they can use it today.

So you're about to purchase a new driver or set of irons. Whether the clubs come from a pro shop or store not on course property, make sure to be properly fitted. For such high prices, new clubs should come with a money-back promise that if the buyer doesn't pass PGA or LPGA Tour Qualifying School, they can be returned. Just because new clubs feel good in your grip, there isn't a guarantee they'll be better than your current set.

To be competitive in today's market, most golf stores have at least one full-scale hitting net on site. They have employees who understand the golf swing and club fitting. If you're buying a club from a store without either service, it's like going for the par-5 in two with water surrounding the green. There is more risk than reward in this situation.

Ever see a kid's eyes fixed on the latest gizmo in a toy store? That's you.

Sure, the club looks like the real deal because it's sparkling new and, in your eyes, made to fit in your golf bag.

Why take a chance?

You wouldn't pull a $1,000 business suit off the rack without a professional fitting.

Go to a store where you can test out the equipment and get measured properly. There may even be a PGA teaching professional on duty to consult about a perfect fitting.

What does a store's proper club fitting for a new set of woods or irons entail?

World of Golf manager Eric Blanchini says he first must know about the golfer's playing ability and amount of money to be invested.

"Then we generally talk about if they draw the ball, slice the ball, do you hit a high ball or a low ball," Bianchini says. "We have a net upstairs and generally have them take three clubs. Anymore than that and they are probably going to confuse themselves. We watch them swing a little bit and make recommendations."

Bianchini or someone on his staff will take measurements involving the club's lie angle and the buyer's hands, wrist, and height. "It's not rocket science for fitting," Bianchini says. "We'll find a club that fits right."

A custom order is placed to the company and completed in one to three weeks.

Golf stores are much more than about specialty wedges,

mammoth-sized driver heads, or the latest $10,000 set of Japanese-made irons.

Maybe you're not looking for new clubs. The old blades are working fine, thank you. They simply may need maintenance: a new grip or shaft. Most stores employ someone who handles various club repairs, from replacing grips to reshafting clubs.

City shops entertain regular customers on a weekly and monthly basis. Avid golfers need to restock their golf bag with new balls, clean and soft gloves, and bags of tees. Once or twice a year they may visit for shoes. If you play a lot, it's not uncommon to buy a pair or two every year or at the very least replace worn-out spikes. Every several years you need a new golf bag.

The biggest discrepancy among off-the-course stores is in the clothing departments. All have clubs, shoes, balls, and golf bags, but not all make apparel a primary selling point. So if you're in dire need of golf apparel, including rain gear, and you are not sure the store carries your brand or a wide selection, call in advance.

Apparel can be a major draw. Men want to wear the latest line of shirts worn by their favorite PGA Tour or Champions Tour players after they see the pros hoist their latest piece of hardware. (Strange how today many men don red shirts on Sundays. Who do they think they are, some guy named Tiger?)

It's not as prevalent, but women also can follow suit with LPGA fashion statements. Designers in the women's golf market are making more of an effort to have their clothing be fashionable both on and off the course.

These stores also vary in supply when it comes to accessories.

Travelers may need a sturdy travel bag. Collectors may want to collect a photo of their favorite player that's autographed and neatly framed. Readers may want to read the latest golfing bestseller or latest step-by-step instructional book authored by David Leadbetter, Dave Pelz, or another one of golf's teaching gurus.

Maybe a trip to the store is for one of those rare golfing purchases: a cherry wood cabinet for showcasing logo golf balls, one of those funny animal headcovers, or the newest self-help gadget to rid players of their slice.

Within all boroughs are avenues for golf at selected shops, municipal course pro shops, and driving ranges. La Tourette and Pelham Bay/Split Rock present the best stocked pro shops among city courses. But, while other municipal courses lack quantity, they may provide specials on items you won't find anywhere else.

Also, if you know which clubs you want to buy and the specifications—shaft flex, swing weight, and grip size—ask your PGA professional if he or she can order them.

Business travelers/golf enthusiasts can stop by two PGA Tour stores at LaGuardia Airport (in the USAir and Delta terminals). For security reasons, the two stores can't sell clubs, but both have favorable selections of golf apparel, books, videotapes, and other novelty items.

Practice facilities at Alley Pond Golf Center, Randalls Island Golf Center, Staten Island Golf Practice Center, and the New York Golf Center at Chelsea Piers have venues with enough equipment to keep potential buyers returning. Ask the staff if you can test demos on site. Some may charge you a small "demo" fee—at the New York Golf Center store at Chelsea Piers it's $5, but the fee is applied to the purchase.

Another alternative is sporting good stores, i.e., Modell's, NikeTown, and Sports Authority. They don't have the wide-range selections of golf specialty stores, but keep them in mind. Especially if you're not satisfied with prices at specialty shops and pro shops at municipal courses and driving ranges.

where to shop

golf country

❋ *2655 Richmond Avenue*
Staten Island, NY 10314
718-761-2068

Golf Country has a deal that has its patrons praying for a major snow day. The "Let it snow" contest means that if it snows six inches or more on Jan. 1, 2005, all December purchases will be 100 percent redeemed with either gift certificates or cash.

For example, someone who buys a $1,000 set of clubs in December should save the receipt in case of a blizzard on New Year's Day. Six inches of snow would create a nice $1,000 windfall. There is no limit to the amount of purchase.

January 2004 marked the store's first contest. Golf Country has an insurance policy in case Mother Nature sides with shoppers.

Located in the Staten Island Mall about a mile from La Tourette Golf Course, the 3,500-square-foot operation carries major club brands as well as apparel, balls, shoes, bags, and accessories. The store has one designated hitting area and a putting green. The staff handles major club repair and fitting. Club cleaning and re-gripping are done quickly on site while customers wait.

Golf Country hours are 10:00 a.m. to 9:30 p.m. Monday through Saturday, and 11:00 a.m. to 6:00 p.m. on Sunday.

golf town

❊ 43-25 Bell Boulevard
Bayside, NY 11361
718-357-2909

www.egolftown.com

Golf Town is located near the busy path of Northern Boulevard, within close proximity to Alley Pond Golf Center and both the Clearview and Douglaston courses.

Most of the major brands of clubs are displayed in the shop. There is one hitting net to test out a possible purchase.

Golf Town has more than an ample supply of golf balls, ranging in price. They also have plenty of golf bags, shoes, but not much in stock when it comes to apparel.

It's open from 9:00 a.m. to 8:00 p.m. Monday through Saturday, and 11:00 a.m. to 6:00 p.m. on Sunday.

new york golf center

MANHATTAN STORE:
❊ 131 West 35th Street
New York, NY 10001
212-564-2255
CHELSEA PIERS STORE:
❊ 62 North River Pier 59
New York, NY 10011
212-242-8899

www.nygolfcenter.com

The Manhattan store located in the Garment District is probably the most impressive of all city shops, in terms of quality and quantity. The first time through the doors there is not enough time for your eyes to focus on everything in this toy store for golfers.

The first floor is massive: wall-to-wall golf merchandise minus the clubs. The New York Golf Center has a large clothing apparel section for men and women. Nike, Ashworth, Polo, Tommy Bahama, and Greg Norman are all here. The New York Golf Center arguably has the largest selection for women, including high-end apparel by Claudia Romana.

There is even an area for juniors, including children's wind shirts.

The store's footwear department doesn't miss a step. Variety in progressive style shoes is aplenty.

Four years ago the store expanded to a second floor, refurbishing a former warehouse area. Steps lead shoppers to an enormous golf club selection. Also upstairs are two hitting nets to test out equipment.

New York Golf Center's Charlie Rhee says his store's location is another reason for its popularity. It's close to Penn Station and across the street from Macy's Herald Square. Originally, the main store was located at 36th Street when it opened in 1983. The store, selected by *Golf World Business* as one of the top 100 golf shops off the course, has been at its present site since 1991.

Manhattan store hours are 10:00 a.m. to 7:00 p.m. Monday through Friday, 10:00 a.m. to 6:00 p.m. Saturday, and 11:00 a.m. to 5:00 p.m. Sunday.

The Chelsea Piers location is a smaller store but one with quality merchandise. One advantage of shopping here is the testing of clubs. Players can try out the clubs at the driving range, getting a better direction of ball flight than when hitting in a net.

Chelsea Piers store hours are 11:30 a.m. to 8:00 p.m. Monday through Friday, 9:30 a.m. to 6:00 p.m. Saturday and Sunday.

northern pro golf

❊ *157-02 Northern Boulevard*
Flushing, NY 11354
718-321-1200

Northern Pro Golf opened its doors in October 2003 and carries a variety of brands, including Japanese manufactured clubs.

One hitting net is on site, but the store doesn't have professional club fitting. There is a club repair section.

A variety of golf bags and solid clothing lines are in the store's mix.

Store hours are from 10:00 a.m. to 8:00 p.m. seven days a week.

panda golf

❊ *9217 5th Avenue*
Brooklyn, NY 11209
718-238-4919

Owners at Panda Golf, adjacent to its sister ski shop, plan to have a hitting net in operation for the spring of 2004. If all goes as planned, club fitting will be on site for customers trying out Callaway, Titleist, and other top-of-the line selections.

Major repair work is available, but handled outside the store. Grips brought in during the morning usually can be picked up the same day, while shaft work may take three days—providing Panda has the replacement in stock.

Panda also has plenty of golf bags, shoes, men and women's apparel, and other accessories.

The store is open from 11:00 a.m. to 7:00 p.m., Monday through Friday, with hours extended until 9:00 p.m. on Thursday. Store hours on Sunday are noon to 5:00 p.m.

paragon sports

✳ *867 Broadway at 18th Street*
New York, NY 10003
212-255-8036
www.paragonsports.com

On the outside, Paragon Sporting Goods Company isn't a "golf store" per se. But a large section devoted to golf lies within the familiar red and black building.

Golfers can find most major brands of clubs, shoes, golf bags, and balls next to a full-swing hitting area to aid fittings. Mizuno, Ping, Callaway, Titleist, Cleveland, and Taylor Made irons appear just like they do at your favorite golf-only store, neatly affixed to club racks on the wall.

Donald Cline, the store's golf aficionado, boasts that Paragon Sports provides almost everything big-time Manhattan golf stores do. Major club repair is about the only golfing service that isn't provided. Cline says the store's heavy attention to golf is similar to its dedication to the skiing market.

Paragon Sports has been in operation since 1908, but Cline says that only in the last five years has it become passionate about selling golf merchandise. Last winter, Paragon Sports expanded the square footage of their golf section.

Located downtown, the store is open from 10:00 a.m. to 8:00 p.m. Monday through Saturday, and 11:30 a.m. to 7:00 p.m. on Sunday.

the world of golf

❊ *147 East 47th Street*
New York, NY 10017
212-755-9398
DOWNTOWN STORE:
❊ *189 Broadway*
New York, NY 10007
212-385-1246
www.theworldofgolf.com

The World of Golf has two well-stocked shops, including the downtown store located a block away from Ground Zero. The other is the East Side's most prominent golf retail shop. Both stores are known for their large collection of new clubs and fitting areas.

At the East Side store, potential shoppers follow a small hallway to the second floor where the entrance is located. To their left they see an impressive assortment of shoes, including a major supply of FootJoys. To the right is a small library of books as well as videotapes. But this store is a major magnet to shoppers because of its room with racks and racks of clubs, from drivers to lob wedges. Hundreds of different styles of putters lean against the wall.

While both stores provide club fitting and hitting nets, the downtown outlet offers a more elaborate station called a launch monitor. It's designed more for the talented golfer, measuring club-head speed, ball speed, path of the club-head, estimated ball flight for drivers, and spin rate for the golf ball.

The downtown store carries approximately the same selection of clubs, but has more men and women's apparel than its East Side venue.

us golf

❊ *41 West 35th Street*
New York, NY 10001
(212) 564-6441
www.theusgolf.com

You may not be familiar with US Golf. You're not the only one. US Golf opened late in 2003, and as this is being written, is looking to add a clothing section.

Golfers are tantalized by a wide-screen television in the store's window, often tuned to the Golf Channel. The store's biggest selling point is its new irons; the store boasts one of the largest selections of Japanese manufactured Honma clubs.

Better check your credit card balance before buying a set of these clubs or even a driver. During US Golf's first three months of operation, a set of Honma irons sold for $10,000.

Certified teaching pros are on staff. One hitting net is upstairs.

The store also carries a good selection of reasonably priced shoes, golf balls, and travel bags.

practice, practice, practice

Practice never makes a golfer perfect. But done correctly, practice can make a golfer better.

A particular golf lesson from my father relates the laws of proper practice. This was one of those days I came home sulking after an embarrassing round. I couldn't get the golf ball airborne. I kept pounding the ball into the turf, even smothering a 5-wood off the tee.

The more I messed up the more stubborn I became.

My dad didn't hesitate returning his pouting son to the course to correct the problem. He immediately recognized my grip was out of whack. But, like many 13-year-olds, I knew more than my father did. At least I thought I did.

Change my grip? That felt too strange. Had to be something else. And, what in Ben Hogan did my father know? He only was a former city champion, a first-round medallist in our state amateur, and had once won two matches in the British Amateur.

Me? At 13, I could shoot in the 50s . . . for nine holes.

I knew more than he did. At least I thought I did.

My signature rut on one of the teeing areas started turning into a near-abyss. I decided to try his advice. Surprise, his grip pointer instantly worked. The proverbial light bulb didn't go off full tilt, but it began to flicker.

Thirty years later I look back at that 13-year-old. Sometimes I want to laugh. Sometimes I want to cry. I know now that kid had a great a teacher to turn to on a daily basis. Yes, I know that now.

Now I want to listen. Now my father's gone. My brother's a teaching pro. Needless to say, I heed his every word.

Where's this going? Whether you're 13 or 113, let me give you some advice. New York City has many certified golf instructors, who, through various career opportunities, have learned from some of the game's greatest teachers.

They're located at city courses, practice centers, and studios. These are their classrooms where they attempt to relay their knowledge.

They offer daily sessions ranging from 30 to 45 minutes to elaborate playing lessons, and provide multi-day single and group packages.

Some can be expensive, but so are the new irons, a year's worth of green fees, and the amount of time invested to play this game. Find the teacher whose price, patience, knowledge, and teaching skills fit your talents.

Then, listen.

Maybe one of these New York City instructors could win your attention. Their careers are surely worth mentioning. So are their teaching tips.

the pros

kelley brooke

❖ Brooklyn Golf Center

Kelley Brooke's career is about getting involved. The LPGA teaching professional is helping oversee a major transition at both the Brooklyn Golf Center and Riis Park Pitch and Putt.

She makes time to teach a little golf. That's good news to her students because Brooke is avid when it comes to introducing new players to the sport, especially juniors and women.

During her playing days she captured the Iowa State High School Championship and went on to an All–Big Ten career at the University of Iowa. In 1992, little did she know she would greatly expand her teaching knowledge by working a year alongside a family friend. That friend turned out to be Butch Harmon, a visible figure in Tiger Woods' success.

"Looking back," she recollects, "I know [working with Harmon] was a big deal."

Brooke adds that "the first two feet of the swing are the most important. The golf swing is a chain reaction, if you get off to a poor start, the chain is broken."

mario calmi

❖ *Alley Pond Golf Center*

Mario Calmi can't seem to escape teaching. Maybe living only a mile away from Alley Pond Golf Center has something to do with it.

"I give a lot of lessons, anywhere from 3,000 a year," says Calmi. "I'm like a machine . . . I don't play in any tournaments and I can't even take a day off."

Calmi was exposed to some of the game's most revered instructors. He spent ten years with David Leadbetter and continues the friendship with one of the PGA Tour's most recognized teachers. Well-known instructors Jim Flick and Jimmy Ballard also were instrumental to Calmi's teaching success.

Long days on the range are worth the time when he sees someone use less effort to hit the ball further. "It's the forearms and shoulders that everyone has problems with," he says. "They're too stiff or too tight. They're looking up and anticipating impact. In a few minutes I have them swinging with their eyes closed."

bill castner

❖ *Turtle Cove Golf & Baseball Complex*

Not many golfers are ardently attached to New York City courses like Bill Castner.

His professional career started in Queens, where for eight years he was an assistant at Towers Country Club in

Floral Park. From there he went to La Tourette for one year and followed with stints at Dyker Beach and Marine Park.

Castner and two other partners purchased the lease on Van Cortlandt from 1987 to 1992, before selling to American Golf. He went on to teach at Randalls Island during its inception. He even worked a week at the Golf Club at Chelsea Piers before deciding the unique complex wasn't for him.

Today, he can be found instructing players at Hyatt Hills Golf Course, a nine-hole facility in Clark, New Jersey. But Castner, known as an excellent short-game technician, teaches one day a week at Turtle Cove in the Bronx. About 50 regular city golfers depend on Castner to keep them in a groove.

"I grew up playing all the city golf courses," he says. "I watched them deteriorate and watched them get better. I like New York City golf. I don't know if I'll ever leave New York City."

young chung
:: *Kissena Park Golf Course*

Young Chung enjoys celebrity status at Kissena Park. He's the neighborhood's VIP: Very Important Pro.

Chung is president of the Korean PGA of the Americas. He's especially proud of his organization's most recognized member, PGA Tour standout K.J. Choi. Walk in the Kissena Park pro shop and it's difficult to miss the picture of Chung and Choi together.

Chung, a 15-year disciple of Bob Toski, heads up his New York Golf Academy from a hitting cage at Kissena Park. Despite a confined classroom, Chung has a large following, including area high school students.

"When you teach students you have to emphasis the grip," he says. "Most of the players don't think about the grip. They're careless."

Each year he returns to Korea as a visiting professor at Kyung Hee University and gives lectures on golf psychology.

"I tell them it's a game of the feel," he says. "Golf is muscular training. I teach them that it's not the physics first. I tell them to feel it first because golf is psychological to them."

paul giordano
❊ *Mosholu Golf Course*

There is plenty of kid in Paul Giordano. Maybe that's why he enjoys supervising Mosholu's popular First Tee program, designed to give all kids a chance to learn the game.

Giordano, a father of three, grew up in the Bronx. He also earned a degree in child psychology from Iona College. So he knows something about kids and growing up in the Mosholu neighborhood.

He's also a PGA teaching professional, having learned alongside beloved playing pros Chi Chi Rodriguez and Doug Sanders. So Giordano has a lot to offer from his head professional position at Mosholu, especially to the younger generation.

"It's kind of like giving back," he says. "This is an area where you can get in a lot of trouble. Kids are mischievous around here. When they're in here, I know they're safe and I know they're having fun. The thing is, they keep coming back.

"We always tell the kids they don't have to come here just to play golf. If they're having a bad day at home they can come up and hang out with us. They can help on the range or hit some balls. We try to encourage the kids to get involved."

john hobbins
❊ *The Sports Club/LA*

Owner of one of the metropolitan area's most esteemed résumés, John Hobbins is equally as interested in a player's fitness as in his or her overall golfing abilities. Hobbins applies strength, flexibility, and nutrition programs to his teaching at the Manhattan club's 330 East 61st Street location (212-207-4552).

"Posture is the cornerstone of my teaching," says Hobbins, who from 1991 to 1999 was the director for Golf Digest's teaching schools and continues to work alongside many VIP instructors. "The way you stand to the ball is going to dictate how you swing your hands and arms, and what plane your shoulders and club will swing. Everything starts with your posture and your setup. What I find is most of my students have no problems integrating the information, once they get good information. They get a lot of bad information, be it on The Golf Channel or through magazines. What they need to understand is that information is only good for the swing model that person teaches. You've got to make sure you have the right information for the way you swing.

"Once you determine that, it's relatively simple as far as applying information."

You don't have to be a member of The Sports Club/LA to receive lessons from Hobbins, whose program includes use of the club's personal trainers. He has a hitting net at the gym and offers a video analysis. Hobbins also works with his students at Randalls Island Golf Center.

A PGA teaching professional for more than twenty years, Hobbins is available for lessons at the club seven days a week, 5 a.m. to 11 p.m. "I market myself as giving the earliest lessons available in the USA each day," he says.

james jond
:: *New York World of Golf*
James Jond says amateurs tend to put all their interests on the driving range in one bucket, so to speak. They spend too much time whaling the big stick.

"My favorite is the short game," says Jond, who for 16 years was the head professional at Willow Ridge Country Club in Harrison, NY. "[I like the idea of] being so near the hole and properly executing the shot. The imagination that you have to have to create is satisfying—great shots around the green and bunkers. Everyone can learn; it's easier to teach someone the short game than hitting the driver."

Jond, who missed by "a few shots" qualifying in the final stage of the 1979 PGA Tour Qualifying School, enjoys his indoor duties at the World of Golf. By hitting into a net and not worrying about ball flight he says it's easier for students to concentrate on fundamentals.

mark lozier

❖ *The Golf Studio*

Mark Lozier grew up in Willoughby, Ohio, where as a caddy he fell in love with the game. That passion led to a career as a golf instructor, watching amateurs discharge shot after shot into a net located in his Manhattan studio at 39 West 32nd Street (212-967-0247).

"I've been averaging over 1,000 lessons (a year)," says Lozier, who developed his teaching skills working three years at the Roland Stafford Golf School. "I'm happy to say the majority of my students are average players. Fifty percent are men and 50 percent are women. They (range from) policemen to firemen to executives. There are a lot of people from the Garment Center.

"It's mostly people trying to break 100 or trying to keep their game in the 90s."

His instructions embrace a better understanding of implementing the arms and body into the golf swing and grip. Lozier, a United States Golf Teachers Federation member, has taught from his studio since 1997.

"I decided I wanted to teach golf to urban golfers," he says. "I set up a space that is devoted entirely to teaching and for my love of the game. I'm not going to get rich doing it, but I'm certainly going to get a lot of satisfaction."

rick nielsen

❊ *Randalls Island Golf Center*

Rick Nielsen's reputation at Ferris State University (Michigan) was that he was the best. For his contributions to the Bulldogs golf team he was named the Collegiate Player of the Year. But he says 20 years on the practice tee is just as satisfying.

"I like teaching more than anything," says Nielsen, the head professional at Randalls Island Golf Center. "I once was a head professional at a club. I owned a shop, but I always taught instead. Then I said I didn't need a shop and gravitated toward teaching.

"I like helping people get better, seeing them get better, and having them get excited about it. It's also about learning new techniques and applying them to help people get better

"That's the most fun."

Nielsen's interest in teaching grew from working with Long Island teaching sensation Mike Hebron. He served as an instructor at Hebron's American Academy for Learning Golf.

nancy platzer

❊ *Forest Park Golf Course*

Nancy Platzer isn't blessed with a big-league practice facility for her classroom. She still finds enough room to teach from a small hitting area on the Forest Park Golf Course.

Her makeshift driving range runs parallel with one of the holes. Regulars usually don't see it as an inconvenience, giving a friendly wave to their Class A LPGA teaching pro.

Her four-day workweek at Forest Park makes her a familiar figure.

Platzer's students should prepare for an old-fashioned workout during one of her hour lessons. They may join her in rounding up range balls via working on wedge shots to the shag bag.

"Basically I work with them on the fundamentals," says Platzer, who for one year taught at Mosholu Golf Course. "I get them on the course quickly. I teach them about the grip, [proper] posture, rules, and etiquette."

For the past three summers she's organized daily junior clinics. Groups consist of three to eight players. Those interested need to call the course in advance.

ed sorge

❖ *Staten Island Golf Practice Center*

Here is someone who knows the sensation of being in a zone. A serious zone.

Ed Sorge believes no one will surpass his seven-under-par 28 at Richmond County Country Club. Sorge's feat came in the quarterfinals of the 1960 Staten Island Amateur. He eventually lost in the finals, but won the tournament the following year.

Sorge also owns the 18-hole scoring mark at La Tourette Golf Course. That day he shot a 64 and defeated then La Tourette pro and future Champions Tour player Jim Albus by five shots.

But Sorge says he expects his 64 will soon be toppled.

"Since about 1975 at La Tourette, over two million people have been trying," says Sorge, who left Silver Lake in 1988 after 22 years as its head professional. "It's been challenged."

One of his neighbors nearly matched Sorge's record. Vin Truscelli, who teaches alongside Sorge at Staten Island

Golf Center, came within one shot of tying the La Tourette course record.

tom sutter

❖ *Golf Club at Chelsea Piers*

Tom Sutter needs less than ten seconds to get his students' attention. All he has to do is tell them he played in the 1998 U.S. Open at The Olympic Club. "You do have an advantage when the student really believes in what you're doing," says Sutter. "You have a commitment to it before the lesson is started."

Sutter carded a two-day total of 152 (79/73) and missed the cut by four shots. Other notable stops in his playing career were the Australian Open, South African Open, PGA Tour's Buick Classic, and Cannon Greater Hartford Open.

He is the head teaching professional at Chelsea Piers. One of his most famous pupils is New York City mayor Michael Bloomberg.

Based on his experience, who has Sutter found to be the easiest golfer to teach? Stickball players. One of his stickball students needed only "two to three years" to break 80.

"I jokingly say that I'm the only pro in the country who would know that because I've taught enough stickball players," he says. "Stickball, of all the sports, works the best for golf. The broom or stick they're using is light, the same weight as a golf club. You have to step through (the ball). The weight shifts are great. . .I can't believe how good stickball players play."

leo tabick

❖ *Staten Island Golf Practice Center and Golf Country*

Teaching peer Bill Castner is quick to name the best swing teacher in New York City. He says hands (and arms and shoulders) down, it's Leo Tabick.

"My methodology is based on the design of the golf club, standing on the inside of the target line, and [the student's] personality, hand-eye coordination, and timing," says Tabick. "And then I use the golf course."

He says his biggest thrill is when someone's "eyes light up" after they get the golf ball airborne for the first time. Tabick continues to teach beginners and other players at the Staten Island Center. From December to March he also teaches from his studio at the Golf Country retail store in the Staten Island Mall.

Tabick's former stints at New York City courses include South Shore, La Tourette, Van Cortlandt, and he was the director of instruction at the Randalls Island Golf Center.

the facilities

You can have the desire to practice. But you also need some place to practice that desire.

I've envisioned Central Park as a great practice area. Imagine the limitless hitting areas in Sheep Meadow. Or perhaps 100 heated stations atop the running track surrounding the reservoir so players can hit iron shots to island greens sprinkled in various spots. Don't touch Belvedere Castle . . . that would be the ideal clubhouse.

Protesters already are knocking at my door. Before they can draw for a pencil attached to a clipboard full of petitions, I'm realistic enough to know that in our lifetimes there never will be groups blasting practice balls in Central Park. Well . . . Maybe Tiger Woods, Annika Sorenstam, and Michelle Wie.

In the meantime, there are practical practice alternatives in New York City free from uproars. Two par-3 courses can be used to develop a better short game.

Within New York City are many practice facilities and several have extensive features.

Some of them have PGA-certified instruction to go along with video analysis, junior clinics, and group teaching. Many offer special discounts, extended passes, as well as designated short-game areas for chipping, putting, and bunker play.

A lot of these facilities are lit for players to work on their games close to the midnight hour and have covered areas with heaters, making it easier to swing away in the wintertime. Many have targets to give players an "on the course" sensation and provide natural grass teeing areas.

Best of all, there are so many that at least one will be located near you.

alley pond golf center

❊ *232-01 Northern Blvd at 234th Street*
Douglaston, NY 11363
718-225-9187

www.golfandsportsinfo.com

All aboard: Take the number 7 train up to the last stop, Main Street. From there, add a thirty-minute bus or cab ride.

Driving along humming Northern Boulevard you hear distracting, repetitive "ping" noises. That's a beautiful and familiar sound to avid golfers, because it means that Alley Pond Golf Center is getting closer.

It's known to be one of the borough's busiest practice facilities, with 75 hitting areas. As many as 30 of those stalls are covered and heated for winter.

"At one time the most balls were hit there than any range in the country," says Tom Sutter of Chelsea Piers.

Alley Pond is so engaging, the tire store across the street has clubs for its patrons to borrow while they're waiting.

"Generations of players have hit balls at Alley Pond," adds Bill Castner. Players pay $7.50 for 85 balls or $10 for 153. Rates are reduced for senior citizens and junior golfers. Rental clubs are available for $2.

The lighted facility is open seven days a week, 6:00 a.m. to midnight in the summer, and 7:00 a.m. to 11:00 p.m. during the winter. The day's last golfers are permitted to hit their first ball an hour before closing.

Early-bird specials—to noon on weekdays, until 9:00 a.m. on weekends—allow golfers more bangs for their buck. Frequent visitors will want to consider the $100 Eagle Book, 12 large buckets of balls for the price of 10.

Alley Pond has a staff composed of English- and Korean-speaking teaching professionals. Head professional Dale Spina has taught in the metropolitan area for more than 20 years. He and a veteran staff tutor one-on-one and small groups, from beginners to scratch players. Lessons for groups are scheduled between May and September and vary from a one-day school to seven one-hour lessons. Nine-hole playing lessons are available and must be scheduled in advance so pros can call ahead to area courses.

On site are a snack bar and pro shop with major brands of golf clubs, balls, shoes, bags, and gloves. Alley Pond also has two 18-hole miniature courses. Adults pay $5.50 and cost for kids and senior citizens is $4.

bronx golf center

✣ *1825 East Gun Hill Road*
Bronx, NY 10469
718-379-6666

All aboard: Take the number 5 train to Gun Hill Road. A short bus or cab ride follows.

Parents can send their kids to camp without sending

them too far away from home.

The Bronx Golf Center, a lighted driving range with 45 hitting zones, has a summer junior golf camp for less than $200. The camp entails five two-hour sessions throughout the week. Groups are four to eight students. During the school year there is a clinic that features five one-hour sessions.

The Bronx Golf Center has two teaching professionals who provide a variety of private lesson packages from full-swing analysis to the short game, as well as adult group lessons.

You can visit the Bronx Golf Center without buying a lesson. With the exception of Christmas Day, the facility is open year-round, from 8:00 a.m. to 11:00 p.m. during the summer, and 9:00 a.m. to 9:00 p.m. in the winter. Players can hit 51 balls for $5. There are daily specials: $10 for 153 balls or $20 for 357 balls.

If you are in search of other sporting activities, the center has a miniature putting course and batting cages.

brooklyn golf center

✴ *3200 Flatbush Avenue*
Brooklyn, NY 11234
718-253-6816

All aboard: Take the number 2 or 5 train to the last stop at Flatbush Avenue. From there, take a taxi or the Q35 bus for a 30-minute ride to the course.

Area LPGA instructor Kelley Brooke is the guiding light to brighter days of golf in New York City. Brooke's guidance and investment backing from Global Golf Services, Inc. of Brooklyn are helping build a $1.5 million practice facility.

For the past 20-plus years the government-owned property was home to the Gateway Driving Range. But Brooke says plans are to tear it down and rebuild from scratch. "It's going to be the premier golf facility in the metropolitan area," says Brooke, who for ten years taught at the Staten Island Practice Center. "I guarantee it."

During the transition, the driving range will remain open with 75 hitting areas. The 18-month project has already started, with lights to be in operation by spring 2004. The driving range will be open from 7:00 a.m. to midnight seven days a week, weather permitting. Prices weren't finalized, but range ball costs were expected to be $6 for a small bucket and $10 for a large bucket.

Upon completion, the Brooklyn Golf Center will feature a 3,500-square-foot well-stocked pro shop with a restaurant, a classroom, and babysitting services; 20 target greens, including an island green; a short game area with individual greens for putting, chipping, and bunker shots; an indoor heated practice area with sliding doors to hit outside; 20 grass teeing areas; and 20 heated teeing stalls outside.

The Brooklyn Golf Center will have plenty of instructional opportunities as well as leagues for women, couples, seniors, juniors, and beginners.

The same group will manage the Riis Park Pitch and Putt, formerly Breezy Point Pitch and Putt. The distance between the two facilities is less than a mile.

golf club at chelsea piers

❄ *Pier 59*

23rd Street and the Hudson River

New York, NY 10011

212-336-6400

Golf Academy: 212-336-6444

www.chelseapiers.com/gc

All aboard: Either take the C, E, 1, 6, 9, N, or R train to 23rd Street, and then take M23 bus west to Chelsea Piers, or take any of the previous trains, or the A, 2, 3, 4, 5, Q, or W to 14th Street and then take the M14 bus. There is also taxi pick-up and drop-off by the main entrance.

Manhattan residents really can't complain about a lack of golf on the island. The Golf Club at Chelsea Piers does its best to deliver the ultimate golfing experience without a blade of natural grass.

The Japanese-style four-tier practice facility puts players on a pad where they can launch balls toward the Hudson River. Chelsea Piers has 52 heated stalls, each equipped with an automatic system that tees up every ball. There is an option of hitting off an artificial surface.

Towering nets on both sides steer players to green-like targets. The back of the net is 250 yards from the teeing areas. Drivers are not permitted on the fourth floor because metropolitan-area John Dalys may pop one or two over the net.

"Hitting on a big, wide range is nice and pleasant, but it's not very target oriented," says Tom Sutter, head teaching professional at Chelsea Piers. "It doesn't put demands on you. You don't see the ball hit the side of the fence when you miss one. You don't get that instant feedback of a swing that could be a double bogey. Here, you get that feedback."

Balls are constantly flying seven days a week. Hours are 6:00 a.m. to midnight from April through September, and 6:30 a.m. to 11:00 p.m. from October through March. Sometimes there is a waiting line downstairs for available stalls. Keep in mind Chelsea Piers' busy peak hours are 5:00 p.m. to 10:00 p.m. Monday through Friday, 9:00 a.m. to 9:00 p.m. Saturday, and 9:00 a.m. to 8:00 p.m. Sunday. And, discounts run during off-peak hours.

At the desk, players purchase pre-paid cards for either $20 (80 balls during peak hours; 118 balls during off-peak hours); $25 (100 or 148 balls), $50 (200 or 295 balls), or $100 (400 or 589 balls). The pre-paid card works like a MetroCard.

If players don't hit their limit, they can reuse the card anytime until it's maxed out.

If you don't bring along your sticks, rentals are available: one club is $4; two clubs are $5; three clubs are $6; and a set of ten clubs is $12.

An assortment of specials runs throughout the week. From April through September, early risers are at the range 6:00 a.m. to 9:00 a.m. daily to take advantage of a $25 unlimited ball special. Annual memberships are available.

Chelsea Piers' Golf Academy is located on the third floor and is the office of more than a dozen instructors. Sutter oversees an accomplished staff that includes a former Division I college coach, an LPGA teaching division member, and professionals who have worked alongside golf's VIP instructors David Leadbetter, Jim McLean, Harvey Penick, Hank Haney, Mitchell Spearman, and Mike Hebron.

Instructors work with pupils on the third floor, either outside or inside, where players can even improve their sand technique from a large bunker or watch their swing on tape. The academy oversees many programs: Golf 101, beginning women's clinic and clinic II, Golf I and II schools, and short game and advanced schools. Junior clinics and junior camps are also a part of the academy's busy agenda.

There are two full-swing simulators. Players choose a course—Pebble Beach, Pinehurst No. 2, Firestone Country Club, and Harbour Town Golf Links are four of 36 available courses—and hit balls into a canvas. Sights and sounds of the course are created within the hitting area.

Simulators can be used on an individual ($45 for an hour) or group basis ($90 for a foursome) or during a lesson. Chelsea Piers also uses its simulators for a golf league. Simulators must be booked 48 hours in advance.

The Chelsea Piers staff also regrips clubs. On the first floor, the New York Golf Center has a pro shop, a fully stocked, mini version of its main Manhattan store on West 35th Street. Outside the pro shop is a putting green. Within pitching wedge distance are the Micro Brewery & Restaurant and Rita's Burgers.

la tourette golf course

❊ *1001 Richmond Hill Road*
Staten Island, NY 10306
718-351-1889

All aboard: From Manhattan, take the Staten Island Ferry. From the landing, it's best to spend $15 for a cab instead of taking the bus which will leave you with a half-mile walk up a hill to the course.

La Tourette can boast it's the only 18-hole New York City course with a driving range. It also has the only Nike Golf Learning Center with a group of teachers. Their objective is to encourage more people to become interested in golf.

In business since 2000, it is open from April through October.

The Nike Center has four different levels of classes all titled "Tee It Up." The four levels are for beginners, players who are familiar with the game but need to improve fundamentals, experienced players, and the extremely experienced players who are close to a scratch handicap.

La Tourette offers group lessons for men and women of all playing levels. Classes for juniors begin at ages 5 and 6 and go through 18. Juniors are placed in programs with different levels of ability where, like at school, they try to graduate to the next level.

As for driving range amenities, La Tourette has 37 stations but no overhead covers or heaters for winter practice. It's a full field range with 100-, 150-, and 200-yard markers from two positions. Two fairway cuts make players feel as if they're actually on the course.

The cost is $6 for 60 balls, and $9 for 90 balls. There is an $80 range pass for ten large buckets.

mosholu golf course

❋ *3700 Jerome Avenue*
   Bronx, NY 10467
   718-655-9164
   www.Mosholugolf.com

All aboard: Take the number 4 train to the last stop at Woodlawn. The course is in view.

The Mosholu facility is recognized as much for its designated practice area as its fine-conditioned putting surfaces.

It's home to the First Tee program that instructs all kids on more than just how to hit a golf ball. Mosholu has a designated classroom where teachers and pupils gather.

Dennis Walters, nationally famed paraplegic golf trick artist, has hit balls in front of Mosholu patrons.

Course professional Paul Giordano and assistant Todd Bordonaro have been known to roll out the red carpet for their patrons. Occasionally the two will stop what they're doing, take their video equipment over to a player they don't know, and give him or her a short lesson. At no cost.

Giordano says he likes doing this to increase interest and potentially add to his student list. Different levels of lessons are offered in packages or daily programs. Group lessons for four are available.

The driving range is divided into two areas, with 43 hitting areas off mats at one end and 30 reserved spaces on grass at the far end. Mosholu is without lights and heated stalls, but the property remains open all year, weather permitting. During the season it's open from 6:30 a.m. to 6:30 p.m.

A single bucket of 60 balls is $5. Mosholu sells discount

keys for any amount up to $125. The more you spend on the key the bigger the discount.

— Mosholu also has custom fitting and club repair. There is a snack bar next to the pro shop.

randalls island

> ✤ *1 Randalls Island*
> *New York, NY 10035*
> Range: 212-427-5689
> Instruction: 917-655-1363
> www.golfandsportsinfo.com
> www.randallsislandgolfschool.com

All aboard: For a $10 round-trip fee, Manhattan residents can board a shuttle from 86th Street and Third Avenue (in front of Modell's Sporting Goods) to Randalls Island Golf Center. Shuttles run every 30 minutes, from 3:00 p.m. to 8:00 p.m. on Mondays through Fridays, and from 10:00 a.m. to 5:00 p.m. on Saturdays and Sundays.

Folks at Randalls Island argue they have the best driving range in Manhattan. They claim their lighted facility allows players to enjoy the open air, whereas Chelsea Piers is too confining. The two-tier Randalls Island facility has 82 hitting areas with more than 40 heated stalls.

Four experienced instructors are on property, overseeing golf schools and clinics. They have programs for novice and advanced players, and they have adult and junior clinics.

Prices for balls range from $6 for a small bucket of 51 to $10 for a large basket of 102. There is a special morning rate of $10 for 170 balls and a winter rate (November through February) of $10 for 153 balls. Rental clubs are $2 each.

Players trying to fine-tune their putting stroke or lob shot technique can use Randalls Island's large green and short game area.

During most of the season it's open from 6:00 a.m. to 11:00 p.m. Tuesday through Sunday, and 11:00 a.m. to 11:00 p.m. on Monday. Check with the pro shop for hours during winter months.

Major repair work (regripping, reshafting, and loft and lie adjusting) and club fitting are available. Teaching professional George Yelvington is the local club-fitting expert, having gained experience through helping the PGA Tour, Champions Tour, Nationwide Tour, and LPGA players. Randalls Island's other instructors include head professional Rick Nielsen and Vito Colonna, both with 20 years of experience, and John Connelly, former New Jersey National Golf Club head teaching professional.

The pro shop is stocked full of clubs of all major brands. There also is an ample supply of golf balls, bags and travel bags, and accessories. The shop's apparel is limited to outerwear and shirts.

Inside is a snack bar and outside are batting cages and miniature golf.

staten island golf practice center

2727 Arthur Kill Road
Staten Island, NY 10309
718-317-0101
www.sigolf.com

All aboard: Bus S-74 stops near the corner of Bloomingdale Road and Arthur Kill Road. From there it's a two-minute walk.

This range may be the ultimate perfect fit for New York City golfers.

Among the five teaching professionals on call at Staten Island Golf Practice Center is Class A PGA professional Bill Ryan, who has been chosen as the Golf Digest club fitter of the year three times. Ryan and the rest of the staff are available by appointment.

The lighted center has 40 permanent turf teeing areas, about a dozen of which are heated. There also is a "private" grass hitting section to accommodate 20 players. Golfers pay $175 annually to use this natural surface. But that doesn't include the cost of range balls.

A large bucket of balls is $10 while a small bucket is $6. Club rental fee is $2. There are discounts for senior citizens and there is a frequent golfer program. For $999 players receive 500 tokens and natural surface privileges. Players also can purchase 20 large baskets and get the next one free.

The Staten Island Center is open during the season from 8:00 a.m. to 11:00 p.m., and during the winter months from 8:00 a.m. to 6:00 or 7:00 p.m.

Junior clinics and junior camps of the daily, three-day, and weekly variety are available June through August. Call to inquire about dates.

Short game enthusiasts will be lured to a 10,000-square-foot bent grass putting surface and a 4,000-square-foot chipping green. Owner Douglas Johnston says he designed this unique chipping area to have "every possible lie in the world."

The center's pro shop sells major brands of clubs, bags, balls, and shoes. The Staten Island Center provides full club repairs.

turtle cove golf & baseball complex

❖ *1 City Island Road*
Bronx, NY 10464
718-885-2646

All aboard: Take the number 6 train to Pelham Bay Park. From there it's a $6 to $7 cab ride.

Players come here first to get in the groove before going around the corner to play either Pelham Bay or Split Rock.

Turtle Cove is a lighted facility with 60 hitting areas, including 12 heated stalls. Ten grass areas are designated for players who prefer hitting off a natural surface.

Players can purchase a small bucket (35 balls) for $5, a medium bucket (75) for $8, or a large one (105) for $10. There are two special offers: three large buckets (315) for $25, and from 8:00 a.m. to 11:00 a.m. 175 balls for $10.

In the summer, Turtle Cove is open from 8:00 a.m. to 11:00 p.m., and in the winter from 8:00 a.m. to 6:00 p.m.

Turtle Cove has a snack bar, a batting cage, an 18-hole miniature golf course, and a recreation room.

for kids only

In New York City, or anywhere, kids can always benefit from an opportunity. Give them a chance to hit their first golf ball and maybe they'll enthusiastically swat another and another. . .they deserve that chance.

Paul Giordano gave that one day at Mosholu Golf Course. Giordano was teaching at the Bronx course when six boys, watching through a fence, started hurling sticks and verbal assaults. The Mosholu head pro left his teaching duties, snuck up behind the group, and grabbed a couple of boys by the shirt while the others fled.

He didn't call their parents.

Instead, Giordano let them play.

"I brought them in (the pro shop) and gave them a good talking to," he remembers. "They said, 'We were wondering what was going on.' I said if they were curious they need to meet me here tomorrow and `I'll teach you how to play golf.'"

Both boys returned and Giordano let them borrow clubs to use on the driving range. That's about the time the president of the Mosholu men's club witnessed Giordano's efforts and decided to teach both boys how to putt.

"Somebody finally paid attention to them," Giordano says. "A lot of these kids don't get a lot of attention at home. They come from bad homes or their parents are separated or divorced. Kids grow up really quick around here. They're forced to grow up a little bit.

"At the end of the day they came over, brought their clubs back up to me and thanked me. I told them to come by anytime. They shook my hand and gave me high-fives."

This story didn't end with slaps of skin.

The next day, the two boys came back to the practice green to work on their putting. Their friends who fled before also returned, still throwing sticks at Giordano.

"The two kids on the putting green came out and said, 'Don't throw sticks at our friend Paul,' " Giordano says. "They were like my little protectors. It's a nice story. They went from being tough guys to being really good guys."

Soon enough, the other boys crossed the fence to join their friends. Giordano, too, put clubs in their hands. Today, it's not unusual for the six boys to show up at Mosholu to see their golf pro friend.

Parents take note, opportunities for junior golf are in New York City.

None is more recognized than the First Tee of Metropolitan New York, which provides kids from all backgrounds a chance to experience the game. There is no cost and the only prerequisite is preregistering.

Giordano and his assistant Todd Bordonaro welcomed more than 2,000 kids to the summer 2003 program, where Mosholu supplied clubs and balls. Many metropolitan pros chipped in their services.

Mosholu was packed with First Tee students from 9:00 a.m. to 5:00 p.m. four days a week during the summer. Every hour and a half there was a wave of 50 students. There are weeks when Giordano estimates that maybe 800 kids hit balls at Mosholu.

Some of the golf and life-skills lessons are taught in Mosholu's Lew Rudin Youth Learning Center, named for the late New York City real estate magnate who pushed for the First Tee program in the Bronx. "We try to teach them to improve their social skills as well as their golf skills," Giordano says.

Most driving ranges in New York City have junior camps and clinics available for a fee. Some courses may run specials. Dyker Beach has a Junior Golf Day every August when club members join kids on the course.

In conjunction with the First Tee, the Police Athletic League (PAL) provides extensive summer programs for 7 to 17-year-olds throughout the five boroughs. Parents interested in registering their kids for classes should call their local PAL center. There is usually a small fee.

The PAL golf programs include weekly indoor and outdoor instruction and conclude with a tournament. In 2003, the PAL golf league finished its season with a tourney and barbecue at Mosholu.

There is the City Parks Foundation/New York Parks and Recreation and their summer golf league schedule. In the past, they've provided free junior golf camps for kids 8 to 14 at area parks in all five boroughs. Junior players learn the fundamentals of driving, pitching, and putting. The City Parks Foundation has also teamed up with area PGA professionals to form the Metropolitan PGA Junior Golf Academy. The program is for intermediate to advanced players, ages 10 to 16.

Clinics are a big part of the itinerary of sanctioned events by the LPGA and PGA Tours. Free clinics are usually held at sites to be determined the Tuesday before the Buick Classic at Westchester Country Club in Harrison, the Long Island Classic at the Red Course at Eisenhower Park on Long Island,

and the LPGA Sybase Big Apple Classic at Wykagyl Country Club in New Rochelle.

The Metropolitan PGA Section oversees approximately 70 events on its junior tour. To be eligible, juniors have to pay a membership fee (between $40 and $50) by mid-May. Each event is $20 to $25, including the two-day NYC Junior Championship annually held at Pelham/Split Rock.

For more information, contact the Metropolitan PGA Section office at 914-347-2325.

veterans road driving range

3044 Veterans Road West
Staten Island, NY 10309
718-317-7900

All aboard: From Manhattan take the Staten Island Ferry, followed by a bus to the corner of Arthur Kills Road and Veterans Road. The driving range is about a block away.

Tuesday nights during summer months are made for kids at Veterans Road Driving Range. Junior clinics are reserved during this time as this lighted range has two teaching professionals on duty. To plan ahead, inquire about clinic times.

The Veterans Road Driving Range provides nearly two dozen hitting areas. The year-round facility features 14 winterized stalls. Mats are used in all areas. Players can take aim at targets from 84 to 250 yards. There also is a practice bunker.

The cost is $6 for a small bucket of balls and $9 for a large basket. Ask about the membership program for a discount on a large bucket of balls.

Rental clubs are $1 each. There is no charge to children for rental clubs.

Veterans Road Driving Range summer hours are 8:00 a.m. to 10:00 p.m. seven days a week. During winter it's open from 8:00 a.m. to 5:00 p.m. Take what you've learned at the range to the South Shore Golf Course, a short drive away.

par-3 courses for when you're starting out

flushing meadows pitch and putt golf course

Corona Park
Queens, NY 11368
718-271-8182

All aboard: Take the 7 train to Willets Point. The course is in walking distance.

Flushing Meadows Pitch and Putt Golf Course, built in 1966, is in the backyard of both the National Tennis Center and Shea Stadium. How close? As roars erupted to celebrate a New York Mets victory in the 2000 post-season, simultaneously a golfer rolled in a putt on the 18th hole. The golfer proceeded to doff his hat toward the applause.

Solid players and beginners flock to this 18-hole course and its nighttime play. Flushing Meadows is open throughout the year, but its fairways are illuminated from March through October on holes that measure anywhere from 40 to 80 yards.

During those eight months players can tee off from 8:00 a.m. to 11:00 p.m., with lights out by 1:00 a.m. In the winter they can begin anywhere from 9:00 a.m. to 3:00 p.m.

The cost is $10.50 on weekdays and $11.50 on weekends, while night rates are $13 on weekdays and $14 on weekends. Senior and junior players receive weekday and weekday night discounts. Rental clubs are $1 each.

Players can expect weekend rounds to last two hours, and 30 minutes less on weekdays. The course's snack bar is open only during summer months. There also is an 18-hole miniature golf course.

riis park pitch and putt

❈ *155th Street and The Boardwalk*
The Rockaways, NY 11694
718-474-1623

All aboard: Take the 2 or 5 train to the last stop in Brooklyn at Flatbush Avenue. From there, take a taxi or the Q-35 bus for a 30-minute ride to the course.

A short walk from the boardwalk can lead to a two-hour stroll down the fairways. Riis Park Pitch and Putt is an 18-hole course with holes ranging from 50 to 150 yards.

The course is under new management and is expected to remain open during renovations.

Riis Park Pitch and Putt is making additions by subtraction—removing 50 trees damaged by Japanese beetles. Cosmetic renovations and the addition of lights will give the course a new look. Riis Park Pitch and Putt is expected to remain open near midnight every night.

As this is being written, investor Global Golf, Inc., hasn't set green fees. Prices are expected to be close to the 2003 rates of $9 during weekdays and $12 on weekends.

the city courses

NOTE: Courses managed by American Golf and New York City Parks allow players to obtain tee times online. First, players must call 718-225-4653 between 8:30 a.m. and 2:30 p.m. Monday through Friday to receive access and pin numbers. They then can go online at www.NYCTeeTimes.com. American Golf provides a phone reservation system (718-225-4653) for its courses. The city is considering installing a one-stop phone reservation system for all 13 courses.

During midweek in late spring, summer, and fall, New York City golfers religiously peck the telephone numbers of their favorite municipal golf course to try and secure a weekend tee time for the following week.

While these green fees aren't your mom and dad's prices, they're still the best rates around. Yes, green fees of late have increased and we have heard complaints at more than one course. Good news is that they likely won't be raised this season. In 2003 to walk on the course, both literally and figuratively, New York City residents (with their $6 annual card) paid $34 on the weekends, $28 on the weekdays before 1:00 p.m., and $25 after 1:00 p.m.

Other 2003 rates and miscellaneous costs included:

- Weekend twilight rate ($15.50)
- Weekday twilight ($14)
- Early morning nine holes weekends and holidays ($15.50)
- Early morning nine holes weekdays ($14.50)
- Senior (62 and over) weekdays ($14)
- Junior (17 and under) weekdays ($7.50)
- Power cart ($14 per person); twilight ($10 per person)
- Pull cart ($4.50)
- Season locker rental ($45)
- Reservations ($2 per player)
- Parking ($2)

American Golf manages the most city courses, including

Clearview, Dyker Beach, La Tourette, Pelham Bay/Split Rock, Silver Lake, South Shore, and Van Cortlandt. Ask about the group's New York Golfers Club Membership where annual dues earn discounts on green fees and four rounds at participating courses.

In 2003, first-time members paid $99 (renewals were $79) and received a Monday through Thursday green fee for Beaver Brook Golf Club (Clifton, New Jersey), Long Island National Golf Club (Riverhead, New York), The Golf Club at Mansion Ridge (Monroe, NY), and either their American Golf home course or twilight time at Long Island National. The dues, which last for 12 months from purchase, also included city course discounts and a USGA handicap card.

City courses are for everyone. When we say everyone, we mean nearly everyone.

An estimated 1 million golfers reside within the metropolitan area, from tournament-seasoned amateur to beginner. While New York City tee time sheets are filled to capacity nearly every day—especially in the summer—players, with patience, can get on course.

"My favorite part is you can have millionaires playing with guys on social security," says Paul Sliva, a professional at Van Cortlandt Golf Course. "It's something I see all the time. Once you get out on that golf course there is no class, no money. Everyone is the same, they're all golfers."

More courses are in demand; Marine Park in 1964 was the last public course to open in New York City. It is strange that it's worked out that way. The exciting news is that a new course finally will be added to the baker's dozen. Ferry Point, a Jack Nicklaus signature layout, will welcome public play to its fairways no later than the summer of 2006.

Expect continued extensive alterations to certain earmarked courses. New financial deals to manage Clearview, Douglaston, Dyker Beach, La Tourette, Pelham Bay/Split

Rock, and South Shore were in place by early 2004, guaranteeing more than $180 million in rent revenue and capital improvements during the next years. Upgrades to those seven layouts and their facilities start this year.

City courses are moneymakers, but not if they're in lousy shape. The overall condition of city courses noticeably improved when former mayor Rudy Giuliani designated $15 million to install computerized irrigation systems and other renovations.

With an enormous amount of play comes wear and tear issues. So upkeep and improved conditions are a must if the masses are expected to keep coming back.

After all, a lot of golfers rely on their city courses.

bronx

mosholu golf course

✣ *3700 Jerome Avenue*
Bronx, NY 10467
718-655-9164
Yardage: 3,253 (Blue markers); 2,534 (Red).
Par: 35.
Architect: John Van Kleek, redesign by Stephen Kay.

All aboard: Take the number 4 train to the last stop, Woodlawn. The course is in view.

If I had only a few hours for golf I'd go to Mosholu.

Easy access means it's easy on the wristwatch. The subway lets players out within a short iron to the first tee. Since the course is only nine holes, three hours is plenty of time to complete the round and quickly catch the downtown subway.

Mosholu, an Algonquin Indian name for "smooth stones" or "small stones," is worth playing for another reason: it's a formidable test for all levels of players. Legendary professional Chi Chi Rodriguez played here en route to nearby family visits. You'll need to strike the ball as consistently as Chi Chi to topple Mosholu head professional Paul Giordano's course record, 31.

Tree-lined fairways, traditionally solid putting surfaces, and several challenging holes underline each player's experience. Simple it's not. Players are tested from beginning to end, concluding with a brutally long par-3. If players want to play the "back nine," they play from slightly different markers designated for second nine use.

"It's not a golf course where you play very aggressively," says Tom Sutter, head teaching professional at Manhattan's Chelsea Piers. "You have to hit the ball straight and conservatively. It's very difficult. Par is a very good score on that course."

After 2004 Mosholu, originally an 18-hole layout, will undergo major renovations due to the upcoming construction of a filtration plant. Part of the driving range, as well as the clubhouse and first hole, will be affected. Work on Mosholu's new look won't begin until 2008 or 2009.

pelham bay golf course

❖ *870 Shore Road*

Bronx, NY 10464

718-885-1258

Yardage: 6,579 (Championship markers); 6,261 (Middle); 5,474 (Forward).

Par: 71 (Men); 73 (Women).

Architect: Lawrence Van Etten, redesign by John Van Kleek.

All aboard: Take the number 6 train to the last stop, Pelham Bay Park. From there it's a $7 or $8 cab ride.

Golfers who frequent Pelham Bay and Split Rock golf courses have the best of both worlds at these golfing venues.

They can try to tackle Split Rock, the most difficult New York City course, or they can find a more forgiving layout at Pelham. More players opt to play the 1901 built Pelham.

From tee shots to green contour, the two courses are vastly different. If condensed fairways make you feel claustrophobic, you should opt for Pelham Bay. Standing on Pelham's first tee you'll notice a beautiful opening with plenty of space to the right for even an errant shot. Pelham injects a freedom to swing away without worrying about ball direction. Your grip is relaxed as you peer over your shoulder and catch a glimpse of a generous 40-yard wide landing area.

But this course can unnerve players without a deft short game. Ever hear that a distinctively sloped green is where a proverbial elephant is buried? You'll find that true on many of Pelham's bent grass surfaces— elephant burial grounds, perhaps. And nowhere is there a more defined two-tier green than on the short par-4 fourth. In the middle of this narrow green is a three-foot incline that is an extension to a nightmare of a pin placement. So it's not unusual to require three, four, or even five putts on this green.

Beginners benefit from Pelham's lack of bunkers in front of greens, but beware of the steep bunkers—some with five-foot banks—that horseshoe behind many of the putting areas. If you can par both the par-4 13th, with its long approach over a valley, and the par-5 14th, with its demanding uphill tee shot, then you're ready to graduate to Split Rock.

Both course records are 65, both records were achieved in 1963, and New Yorker Richard Carroll owns both record-breaking rounds. Carroll, whose scoring marks can be recognized in the Pelham/Split Rock clubhouse, continues making appearances at the Bronx facility. He also scored a rare feat when he won two amateur tournaments in one day.

split rock golf course

❄ *870 Shore Road*
  Bronx, NY 10464
  718-855-1258
  Yardage: 6,174 (Championship markers); 6,281 (Middle);
  5509 (Forward).
  Par: 71.
  Architect: John Van Kleek.

All aboard: Take the number 6 train to the final stop, Pelham
Bay Park. From there it's a $7 or $8 cab ride.

Meet the beast of New York City golf courses: Split Rock.
"It's like [the turnaround] at Bethpage Black," says Bill
Castner, "If they ever got it in shape, they could play a U.S.
Open at Split Rock. It's just that good."

Others, too, see the potential. Within the next three
years, the city and American Golf will attempt to transform
Split Rock into a tournament-quality course. Well-known architect Robert Trent Jones Jr. will oversee a renovation project.

The idea is to lure a recognized tourney to the course,
possibly a USGA event, says one American Golf official.

Split Rock could provide a solid tournament atmosphere.

Picture hole after hole where players have to maneuver
shots with only 15 to 20 yards of landing space. Limbs from
tall oaks overhang many of the fairways and cruelly shrink pas-
sageways to Split Rock's greens. Making matters more
difficult are subtle elevation changes to the greens. If you're
playing Split Rock for the first time, it's best to consider
choosing one more club to reach the greens.

Tradition rules at the Split Rock property. The par-5 fifth is
one of Split Rock's most memorable holes. It's reachable in two,
but players may want to back off on aggressive play because of
trouble on both sides of the green. Along the hole is the stone
wall where Col. John Glover in 1776 led 40 colonists during a
key battle against a much larger contingent of British troops.

The history lesson continues on the signature par-4 ninth. Thick limbs from a massive white oak shadow a third of the ninth green. The 350-year-old white oak is one of the five oldest of its kind on the eastern seaboard, and its base is 14 feet in circumference.

The inconsistent overall condition is sometimes not up to par because of drainage problems. But it's improving. If course management or the city wants to, they have enough room to stretch the course to close to 7,000 yards. That might really scare off players, though.

Both Split Rock and Pelham have made a slight change since 2002. General manager Brian Higgins thought it best to flip-flop nines on each course because of a pace of play issue. Players would start slowly because the former starting holes were overly difficult. Thus, the old number ten at Split Rock is now number one, an easier hole (423 yards from the regular tee markers) and more forgiving start.

van cortlandt park golf course

❖ *South & Bailey Avenue*
Bronx, NY 10471
718-543-3114
Yardage: 6,102 (Championship); 5,883 (Middle); 5,388 (Forward).
Par: 70.
Architect: Tom Bendelow, redesign by Stephen Kay.

All aboard: Take the number 1 train to the last stop, Van Cortlandt Park/242nd Street. It is a short walk to the course.

Even if it's not your favorite, Van Cortlandt, which made history with its opening in 1895, has to be on everyone's list of courses to try at least once. It's the only place where golfers can claim afterward: "I played the oldest public golf course in America."

When he wasn't hitting dingers at the "House" he built, Babe Ruth enjoyed hitting the long ball at Van Cortlandt, named for former New York City mayor Jacobus Van Cortlandt. The Three Stooges partook in fun and games here. The course's rich history continues to lure all types of personalities. In accordance with New York City's nature, it's not uncommon for some of the area's big financial hitters to play alongside blue-collar workers.

Soon after a short walk from where the 1 and 9 trains stop or from the parking lot, players are focused on a panoramic view of the modest clubhouse with a serene lake and wooded area in the background. Upstairs are rustic locker rooms—a scene from *Wall Street* was filmed here—where the sun peeks through and adds life to the timeworn place, a good place to stow the clubs instead of regularly toting them on and off the subway.

During summer months, regulars arrive around 5:00 a.m., but never before pro shop employee Margie Davitt, who positions herself behind the counter to offer a "good morning" greeting to the day's earliest birds. She gets there first.

Players converge on benches outside the clubhouse as they listen for their respective groups to be called to the first tee, a long jaunt from where they are waiting.

They're about to play one of the city's best-conditioned courses that is not overly difficult, but one with its share of demanding holes. Van Cortlandt has two par-5s more than 600 yards in length. Its four finishing holes are on elevated and heavily wooded property away from the rest of the course. Players often walk off the 14th green for their final hole of the day. It's worth the trip to play Van Cortlandt's most picturesque stretch. Three of the four are risk-reward par-4s (tip: don't use the driver on numbers 15 and 16), while the 17th is a slightly uphill, long par-3.

"When you think of a public course you think of hitting it anywhere," Sutter says. "But it's a tight golf course. You have to be ready to play."

Etiquette 101

Golf in the city involves a lot of people.

Some view that as a major hindrance. There are worse problems . . . like tee markers unknowingly set by course superintendents that align players out of bounds.

Seriously, try to look in a positive manner at New York City's abundance of play.

You know the adage about the cup being half-full or half-empty? So a long day on the golf course beats a bad day on the clock.

Appreciate that so many people have the desire to play your game. More importantly, be glad they have the opportunity to play this game. That can't be said for a lot of other places.

Say what you want, golf in New York City is for everyone. The deafening roars and unparalleled fervor at Bethpage during the U.S. Open may have come off as obnoxious to outsiders. Four years ago I would have thought they were.

Now I understand.

Staunch, passionate support is a way of life here . . . especially after September 11th, 2001.

It's similar to the day-to-day working scenario we encounter in Brooklyn, the Bronx, Manhattan, Queens, and Staten Island. Go to any city course, and they're all there: women and men, all races, all religions, young whippersnappers to 80-something veterans, rich and poor.

Any three combinations of the above could wind up next to your name on any city course tee sheet.

Prepare for a five-hour round. Enjoy the stroll on the fairways. You may walk upon a view in the distance where life is not so slow, possibly of the Manhattan skyline or the Verrazano-Narrows Bridge.

Here are ideas that could help the round go a little quicker and a lot smoother:

*Turtles let the hares pass: Many times a group is so caught up in the competition they forget about the foursome behind waiting on every shot. If there is a hole open in front, wave the quicker group through.

*Tick tock, tick tock: Ever had playing partners read a putt as if they're a sixth-grade geometry teacher performing at the chalkboard? Do they ever miss an angle? One suggestion is they should line up their putt way before their turn.

*Majority doesn't rule: Some players are too stubborn in their ways and believe that because they're a foursome, they have the right to hold up a twosome or single player. If there is a window ahead, wave them through. It will take less than five minutes . . . about the same amount of time you spent looking over that putt on the previous hole.

*Help out the course super: Have you ever maintained a course after 60,000; 70,000; or 80,000 golfers? That's what city course superintendents and their staffs do every year. Help out. If you see a messy bunker, give it a once-over with a rake. On the green, fix your ball mark and someone else's.

*Only the shadow doesn't know: This is usually only the fault of beginning players. Their shadow is in the line of someone eyeing a putt and it becomes a distraction.

*Draggin' along: If the greenskeeper acts as if someone spit in his morning coffee, it may be because many players are dragging their feet on his fine groomed greens. Wearing non-metal spikes doesn't make a difference when an average of 600 feet tramples a green per day. Pick up those feet.

*Too close for comfort: You're going to wait during some point in the round for the group ahead to clear the green. But don't hit your approach shot just as players leave the green. Wait until their carts are gone or they've walked safely away to the next tee.

*Dress code: Never wear plaid pants and a striped shirt on the golf course. (Did my wife put this suggestion in for someone in particular?)

*Ladies, too: Speaking of wives, never drive past the red tees forgetting they need to hit their tee shots. That doesn't go over too well.

*Long course, long day: Leave the ego home. Don't play the back tees, for example at Split Rock or La Tourette, unless you're good enough or have accepted the fact you're in for a long day. If it's the latter, take a good look at the group behind you. You're sure to hear from them during your round.

brooklyn

dyker beach golf course

    ❊ *7th Avenue & 86th Street*
    Brooklyn, NY 11228

    718-836-9722

    Yardage: 6,504 (Championship markers), 6,260 (Middle), 5,696 (Forward).

    Par: 71 (Men), 72 (Women).

    Architect: Tom Bendelow, redesign by John Van Kleek.

All aboard: Take the R train to 95th street, followed by a cab or bus ride or 20-minute walk.

Half the fun of playing Dyker Beach isn't making birdies and pars. It's listening to stories from Dyker Beach regulars.

These lovable locals never leave the golf course. They break at nightfall and come back in the morning to tee it up and shoot the breeze or play cards—likely both—on one of many picnic tables. Dyker Beach truly is their second home.

Meet Angelo Cella, 66. Two days each week he wears a ranger's cap and directs players around the course. Count on this retired court reporter being there the other five days of the week taking in the camaraderie with his pals in the Sand-trappers Club, an organization made up of senior men at Dyker Beach. As a kid, Cella caddied, shined shoes, and cleaned clubs at Dyker to help pay for his college education. He vividly recalls Dyker being a popular spot for the Brooklyn Dodgers, especially Hall of Famer Pee Wee Reese.

Joe Finn, 83, is another part-time ranger and longtime member of the Sandtrappers. Finn retired in 1972 from his local routes as a driver for Field's meat company. "Nobody ever retired broke like I did," he quips. He takes great pride being one of the course's unofficial historians. He knows that near the sixth is where the FBI came in the early 1990s in search of bodies. Accounts of stolen cars that ended up on the course are a part of his memory.

"I would say they are all true," says Jeff Contrady, the Dyker Beach head professional for the past ten years about these stories. "I was here and lived through most of 'em. It wouldn't surprise me if on any given day the coroner's office showed up with a shovel out here to dig for something they think is out there."

Those were the bad old days.

Dyker's most recent non-golf story came in 2003 when Hurricane Isabel destroyed many trees. Trees or no trees, there is plenty of golf to be played at Dyker. The course used to be the most-played venue in the city and today maintains its popularity. It's a favorite because its greens are usually in solid condition, it provides stunning views of the Verrazano-

Narrows Bridge and the old-fashioned tower at Poly Prep Country Day School, and it has traditionally strong fields in its Memorial tournament. "My favorite is the [par-4] fifth hole [because] when you stand on the tee you see the Poly Prep clock tower," says Carol Fontana, who grew up playing on Dyker Beach and is president of its women's association; "it looks very countryesque."

To Fontana, Dyker always has been a popular hangout. She used to sleigh-ride down Dead Man's Hill on the 8th hole and ice skate on the 5th and 13th holes. She remembers her father waiting in line with other players near the first tee, all sitting in chairs. And today, Finn says, it's not uncommon for players, an hour or so before dusk, to pay full green fees to try and get in as many holes as possible. Another believable tale associated with Dyker Beach.

marine park golf course

✣ *2880 Flatbush Avenue*
Brooklyn, NY 11234
718-338-7149
Yardage: 6,866 (Championship markers); 6,609 (Middle); 5,323 (Forward).
Par: 72.
Architect: Robert Trent Jones.

All aboard: Take the number 2 or 5 train to the last stop, Flatbush Ave., then take the Q-35 Green bus or a taxi to the course.

Robert Trent Jones is one of golf's most respected architects. No wonder the mention of his name gives Marine Park's layout instant credibility. In 1964, Jones made use of this former landfill by the ocean to provide Brooklyn with an inviting links style course. Make that a long, links-style course.

No municipal course in New York City is longer. Constant winds make the nearly 7,000-yard course longer than it actually is. It's not uncommon for 20- to 30-mile-per-hour after-noon winds to push players throughout their round. But this can provide a sentimental journey. The ocean breeze and other links qualities are commonplace every July at the British Open.

Early survival is pivotal to scoring well at Marine Park, where the lowest recorded round is a 66. Players can get dis-couraged with numbers two and three, two lengthy par-4s that usually are played into a prevailing wind. The whole course isn't played against the wind. Mother Nature begins to assist players on the short 335-yard par-4 fourth. From this fairway, players can peer ahead and see the Empire State Building and be reminded they're no longer in Scotland or England.

The rest of Marine Park isn't as difficult as its early holes or the 459-yard 15th. Marine Park is wide–open—there is no real distinction between fairway and rough—and players can use a bump-and-run approach to many of the course's large greens.

An ideal finish takes place near dusk when players can catch a glimpse of the sunset while ending on the par-5 home hole. It's a place to inhale the ocean breeze before returning to city life. Upon heading back to the clubhouse, you'll notice nearby a tasteful memorial for 9-11 victims, decorated with small American flags.

queens

clearview golf course

❧ *202-12 Willets Point Boulevard*

Queens, NY 11360

718-229-2570

Yardage: 6,470 (Championship markers); 6,257 (Middle); 5,676 (Forward).

Par. 70.

Architect: William H. Tucker.

All aboard: Take the number 7 train to Main Street, then the Q-16 bus or a taxi to the course.

Clearview is a popular place. Perhaps it's too popular. In 2002, more rounds of golf were played on this course than on any other course in the city, or possibly anywhere. Clearview recorded 87,046 rounds during 2002, nearly 18,000 more than its closest 18-hole competitor, Dyker Beach. If you schedule a tee time for Clearview, make sure to bring plenty of patience.

Why so busy? It's the home course for a thriving Bayside community, and it's close to the Bronx, Queens, and Long Island. Being off the first exit when entering Queens from the Throgs Neck Bridge doesn't hurt. Another factor that draws players is that the course is wide open, making it attractive to beginners.

There always is something going on Clearview's tee time sheet. Associations include two weekend clubs, an early bird club, an Asian club, a senior club, two ladies' clubs, as well as time set aside for public and parochial schools.

Clearview, whose restaurant, Cafe on the Green, is in the former home of silent movie icon Rudy Valentino, is aptly named because of its never-ending panoramic views. Playing the downhill par-4 17th, players will want to stop to take a picture with the Throgs Neck Bridge and Long Island Sound in the background. On the course, Clearview's other signatures are its small greens and the stretch of holes numbers 14 through 17.

douglaston golf course

❊ *63-20 Marathon Parkway*
Douglaston, NY 11363

718-428-1617

Yardage: 5,585 (Championship markers); 5,140 (Middle);
4,602 (Forward).

Par 67.

Architect: William H. Tucker, redesign by Robert Bruce
Harris and Frank Duane.

All aboard: Take the Long Island Railroad to Douglaston Station. From there it's a four- to five-minute cab ride.

Expect a different Douglaston Golf Course for 2004 and beyond. Norman Tafet, who manages Forest Park and the Flushing Meadows Pitch and Putt Golf Course, and his son Michael took over operations in January when their group signed a 20-year contract. They've already earmarked $3 million for course renovations and another $2 million to improve the facility's restaurant.

Stephen Kay will supervise the renovation project. In the interim, the 550-yard par-5 closing hole will be divided into two short par-4s. The 19 holes mean Kay and his team can work on a specific hole while golfers still play 18.

Upon its completion in the spring of 2005, Douglaston will be ornamented with refurbished teeing areas, bunkers, and greens as well as improved drainage and a new clubhouse. And, the 18th will return to its familiar par-5 look.

"There may be times players will be teeing off of temporary tees," Norman Tafet says about the transition period. "(But) there will be the least amount of inconvenience for the golfer."

Construction won't bury Douglaston's tradition and characteristics.

Being close to Aqueduct, Belmont, and Jamaica racetracks made it a favorite course for two-time Triple Crown–

winning jockey Eddie Arcaro. New York Yankee great Babe Ruth frequently played Douglaston.

Ever wonder about how to handle a pre-shot routine in front of a gallery? Imagine no more. Douglaston offers such a—gulp!—"Tournament" experience. The first tee is within a whisper from the practice green where it's not unusual for 10 to 20 players to stare while waiting their turn. They'll stop their pre-round routine to focus on players beginning their day on the wide-open par-4.

First tee-jitters isn't the only obstacle. Players learn the hard way that Douglaston's turf doesn't serve up many flat lies. And because of so many blind-shot encounters, along with seven par-3s and small greens, course knowledge is worth three or four shots. At least.

If you can manage uphill and downhill angles you'll find Douglaston to be a rather easy course. The unique par-67 layout (when the 18th is a par-5) has three consecutive par-3s (Nos. 15–17).

Built in 1927, it's a short course that demands only a minimal walk from each green to the next tee. At the end of the day players can dine at Douglaston's on-site facility, hosted by restaurateur Dominick Bruccoleri and the facility's culinary team.

forest park golf course

❖ *101 Forest Park Drive*
Queens, NY 11363
718-296-0999
Yardage: 6,053 (Championship markers); 5,635 (Middle); 5,300 (Forward).
Par: 70 (Men); 72 (Women).
Architect: Tom Bendelow, redesign by John Van Kleek and Lindsay Ervin.

All aboard: Take the J train to Forest Parkway. The course is a half-mile up the hill.

Forest Park is beginning to grow due to its past improvements. It's definitely vaulted recently within the New York City golf market.

The current ownership has a lease on Forest Park through 2014 and made a big difference when it opened a new clubhouse in 1997. "There was no bathroom and no facilities," says Bob Smith, Forest Park golf director. "We probably doubled the amount of rounds. With the new irrigation system the course is fully green from tree line to tree line. It used to be green down the middle."

Course owner Norman Tatet recollects, "Ten years ago when I came here there were seven abandoned cars on the course."

Smith has seen the course progress from when he used to shag balls as a ten-year-old. He recalls the course getting smaller and smaller because of nearby road construction. But he says the changes of late have been for the best.

The layout also underwent a recent facelift, with refurbished teeing areas. Forest Park became a more formidable course when the fourth hole was lengthened and converted into a par-5. While the course remains short on paper, it requires more than a handful of accurate tee shots.

"It's very, very tight—off the tee and on second shots," says Smith, whose personal Forest Park best is a 64, two shots shy of the course record. "Half the course you have to hit accurate tee shots."

Players will discover Forest Park's back nine is more of a challenge, including a tough stretch from 10 to 15. The par-3 15th is an innocent 145 yards, but can be a tricky carry over water, thanks to a prevailing one-club wind.

Summer is always the busiest time at Forest Park, where Smith estimates 90 percent of the rounds is from regulars. "I call it the country club," says Forest Park teaching professional Nancy Platzer. "People are really friendly and the course is in good shape." The locals usually start showing up an hour before sunrise. Golfers in the summertime can enjoy additional activities in Forest Park, like hiking, horseback riding, and weekend concerts at nearby George Seuffert Sr. Bandshell.

kissena park golf course

✳ *164-15 Booth Memorial Avenue*
Flushing, NY 11365
718-939-4594
Yardage: 4,665 (Championship markers); 4,389 (White); 4,087 (Red).
Par: 64.
Architect: John Van Kleek and redesign by Stephen Kay.

All aboard: Take the 7 train to Main Street and Q-65 Queens/Nassau bus to the course, or E train to Parsons Boulevard and Q-65 bus to the course.

Driving on Booth Memorial Avenue you may see an establishment called "On in One Sports Bar and Grill." Open its doors and it's as if you've left Queens and wound up in an English pub, with frolicsome patrons and a talkative bartender projecting above the sound of the television. But this lively gathering isn't leading cheers for Manchester United or Arsenal. Instead its support is thrown to the Giants or Jets.

Beyond the noise is a peaceful, hilly meadow. But in no way does it go unused. This is Kissena Park, a unique par-64 where regulars boast their course has the best any city layout can offer. The best views. The best par-3. And, the best course for seniors.

Seniors continue to be in love with this course, says pro shop attendant Al Fioravanti. He'll hear mutterings of elder players failing to break 100 or 150, but he notices they return soon for another shot. The par-4 sixth is senior friendly, with only 314 yards to a double-tiered green. It's one of seven par-4s that measures less than 320 yards from the middle tees. There are eight par-3s and no par-5s. But Kissena Park's many hills make the course feel longer than it is.

The course scores high marks on two holes. The par-3 ninth is a 184-yard bear of a hole for players of any age. So elevated is the green it's difficult to gauge pin placement. Locals brag the teeing area on the 11th is the highest point in Queens. They claim there is a panoramic view of Manhattan like no other.

Fun never seems to end at the course or in the grill. There is the Kissena Park Golf Club run by Fioravanti and some of his buddies, where, even in October, club members are in the grill hotly discussing scores from the day's tournament. Now whether they could hear their golf talk over commotion for the city's two pro football teams is another story.

staten island

la tourette golf course

❊ *1001 Richmond Hill Road*
Staten Island, NY 10306
718-351-1889
Yardage: 6,692 (Championship markers); 6,322 (Middle); 5529 (Forward).
Par: 72.
Architect: David L. Rees, redesign by John Van Kleek and Frank Duane.

All aboard: From Manhattan, take the Staten Island Ferry. It's best to spend $15 or so for a cab instead of taking the bus—the nearest stop is a half-mile walk up a hill to the course.

Split Rock may be New York City's sternest golf test. Van Cortlandt is the oldest. But in the middle of Staten Island's postcard Greenbelt setting, La Tourette, with its Nike Golf Learning Center and magnificent restored clubhouse, arguably is the area's most beautiful golf experience.

The classic layout is boasted by many to be the area's best overall course, if not *the* best. No two holes are alike, says former La Tourette professional Bill Castner. It's layout continues to withstand time, i.e., golf balls that travel further than ever and the high-tech clubs that launch them into orbit.

La Tourette's final stretch is worth waiting for: four finishing holes, three par-4s and the 497-yard par-5 17th. Players must overcome a blind shot on the 394-yard 15th and difficult tee shots on the 397-yard 16th and 398-yard home hole. One of the best views of the area is from the elevated tee on the par-3 7th. And surrounding the course are two hiking trails through the Greenbelt.

"When you play La Tourette, you don't think you're in the City of New York. You clearly don't," says Steven Zuntag, director of the New York City Amateur, annually held at La Tourette. "It's really in the middle of the Greenbelt in Staten Island. It's a great layout. Even with all the new equipment, it stands the test of time."

A Nature Center is scheduled to be unveiled in 2004 that will further preserve the Greenbelt area and at the same time provide additional activities for sightseers. The only reminder you're in the city, meanwhile, is the long wait on Richmond Hill Road while trying to turn left into the La Tourette parking lot.

When first-time players arrive they can't help but be fascinated by La Tourette's historic three-story brick clubhouse. The La Tourette House is a New York City landmark that was restored following a major fire in 2001. A bit of golf history is inside, between the pro shop and the snack bar. A collection of memorabilia reveals some of La Tourette's rich history. There you'll discover Champions Tour player Jim Albus was once its head professional; former longtime Silver Lake pro Ed Sorge holds the La Tourette record with a 64 in 1975; golfing legend Arnold Palmer was on hand for the course's 15th anniversary of the March of Dimes Celebrity Golf Championship.

silver lake golf course

❖ *915 Victory Boulevard*
Staten Island, NY 10301
718-447-5686
Yardage: 6,150 yards (Championship markers); 5,745 (Middle); 5,200 (Forward).
Par 69.
Architect: John Van Kleek.

All aboard: From Manhattan, take the Staten Island Ferry. The course is a five-minute cab ride from the landing.

Silver Lake has its flaws, but its former players embrace its existence. Short by today's standards, Silver Lake is no pushover because of its tight and hilly features. It continues to be a perfect fit for the muni player.

Former PGA Tour regular and Staten Island native Bill Britton recalls climbing under or over fences surrounding Silver Lake as a youngster. "We had the run of the place," says Britton, 47. "Playing golf was like going to the park and playing baseball. There were a bunch of guys from the neighborhood. Some nights there would be seven of us out there. We'd play holes five through eight because they were away from the clubhouse. It was in rough condition, but, in a sense, that was good because we learned to hit pitch shots off dirt paths."

Britton went on to play high school golf at Staten Island's Monsignor Farrell, and college golf at Miami Dade North (Florida) Junior College and University of Florida. In 1990 he finished fourth in the PGA Championship and seventh in the

Masters and in 1989 won the PGA Tour Centel Classic. Today he's the head professional at Eagle Oaks golf course in New Jersey. And to think his golf career started by scaling the Silver Lake fence.

Perhaps old hands at Silver Lake still exchange stories about one of its best players sneaking on the course. Locals continue to make the Silver Lake clubhouse their sojourn. Golf lore exudes from a cozy atmosphere with pictures on the wall of Jack Nicklaus, Arnold Palmer, Gene Sarazen, Bobby Jones, and Sam Snead.

Players who haven't reunited with Silver Lake for a while quickly notice a tighter, more accuracy-driven course. No longer are these the small trees that once lined the fairways. Before making a tee time, call the pro shop to see if your round will include a temporary green or two, an inconvenience in the past. Locals say Silver Lake suffers more than other city courses from rough winters, resulting in poor conditions in the spring. But they proudly mention that their 1929 layout always bounces back.

The course's signature hole is the ninth, a short par-4 with out of bounds on the left and a ravine and trees on the right.

south shore golf course

❊ *200 Huguenot Avenue*
Staten Island, NY 10312
718-984-0101
Yardage: 6,366 (Championship markers); 5,897 (Middle); 5,249 (Forward).
Par: 72.
Architect: Alfred H. Tull.
All aboard: From Manhattan, take the Staten Island Ferry and then take the S-74 bus, a 30- to 45-minute ride to the course.

South Shore conjures up a false sense of security: It appears easy in the yardage book, but is challenging in person.

Three relatively short par-4s and two reachable-in-two par-5s catch the attention of first-time players. Check twice the scorecard because South Shore has two monster par-5s, not to mention several par-4s that require long irons or fairway woods to reach the green in regulation.

South Shore, built in 1927, has a good mixture of holes and while it's a short course, it's certainly not a simple one. "The couple of par-4s [numbers three through four, 278 yards and 260 yards respectively from the middle markers] are drivable," says Staten Islander Steven Zuntag, longtime director of the New York City Amateur. "But, if you don't drive the green, you can make five or six. You can have five or six birdies in a round on South Shore and still shoot 75."

The first shot of the day is arguably the most difficult. The opening hole requires players to neatly position their tee shot on this severe dogleg left par-4. Beware of the two par-5s on the front nine: number five, a three-shot test through a valley to the green; and number nine, more than 500 yards with a cruel sloping fairway.

Built during the Depression, South Shore originally was known as a private facility, the Mayflower Country Club. In the late 1940s, the course played host to the Ray Robinson Open, in honor of welterweight and middleweight champion Sugar Ray Robinson. Heavyweight champ Joe Louis was one of many boxers to play in the event.

Some semblance of a country club setting remains, albeit on public property. At dusk, a wedding reception or another get-together may take place on the second deck of the clubhouse, easily within view of players completing the ninth hole.

and two private courses

richmond county country club

❊ *1122 Todt Hill Road*
Staten Island, NY 10304
718-351-0600
Yardage: 6,619 (Championship markers); 6,325 (Middle);
5,577 (Forward).
Par: 71.
Architect: Robert White.

It pays to play this New York City private course. The cost is nearly $50,000 to join Richmond County and receive its family-oriented membership benefits that include access to tennis courts and a swimming pool.

But money isn't the only obstacle to be considered. There is a five- to six-year waiting list. Richmond County has close to 500 members, 300 of whom are "golfing" members.

There is another way to get on one of the country's first 100 golf clubs recognized by the United States Golf Association. It's much easier on your finances. Guest fees range from $40 to $80 throughout the season, but you have to play with at least one member. So find a friend who's a member. It will be worth your time. Unlike Staten Island's busy public golf playgrounds—La Tourette, South Shore, and Silver Lake—Richmond County averages only 22,000 rounds annually.

Richmond County was established in 1888, but it's unknown when the golf course opened. The site of a former U.S. Open qualifier, Richmond County is considered a tricky course. Hills, hills, and more hills define the course. The front nine is predominantly played uphill, while the back nine is mostly downhill. Players hitting off the par-4 10th teeing area are standing on one of the highest points on the eastern seaboard. Quick, severely undulated greens and narrow fairways add to its ticklish nature.

towers country club

✻ *272-86 Grand Central Parkway*
Floral Park, NY 11005
718-279-1848
Yardage: 5,650 (Championship markers); 5,285 (Middle); 5,205 (Forward)
Par: 70
Architect: Wilfred H. Follett, redesign by Frank Duane

Towers Country Club gives added significance to the phrase "home course advantage." Only residents of North Shore Towers enjoy membership privileges to their backyard playground in eastern Queens. Dues include an annual $3,638 fee plus cart rentals ($17 for 18 holes; $11 for nine). Guests pay $40 on weekdays and $45 on weekends and must be accompanied by a member. Towers Country Club's season is from March through December for carts and year round for walking.

The course opened in 1925 as Glen Oaks Golf Club, but today only three holes maintain their original routes. In the mid-1970s it underwent a major redesign by architect Frank Duane following construction of the 33-story, three-tower North Shore complex. Short in yardage, the course keeps players focused with its snug fairways and undulated putting surfaces. Towers Country Club's most striking holes are its par-3 second, a 170-yard test where one tower poses as a mountain backdrop; par-4 seventh, a sharp dog-leg right design to an elevated green; and par-5 12th, a dog-leg left to another perched green. A smidgen of course trivia: 17 holes are in Queens County, but most of the opening hole crosses over the Nassau County border.

Chuck Robbins, president of the facility's board of directors, says the course has approximately 400 members. Speaking of numbers, there are 1,844 units in this co-op facility ranging from $175,000 to $1.5 million. Residents also bask in health clubs, indoor and outdoor pools, and lighted tennis courts.

coming soon!

ferry point golf course

❊ *500 Hutchinson River Road*
Bronx, NY, 10451
Phone number is not yet available
Yardage: More than 7,000 yards from championship markers. Two additional teeing areas will be provided.
Par: 72.
Architect: Jack Nicklaus.

Directions: Driving from Queens, take the first exit off the Bronx Whitestone Bridge.

This course has world-class potential and all the makings to become New York City's finest public layout. From landfill to beautiful links, it's getting closer to being a reality. Finally.

Ferry Point is a Golden Bear signature design, meaning Jack Nicklaus personally had a hand in the development of each hole. The project has been in the works for five years, but at one time it was delayed because of environmental issues. Nicklaus, a part owner, and other Ferry Point officials are back on course and pushing toward an opening in either the spring or summer of 2006.

Course developer Pierre Gagne compares Ferry Point to Ben Crenshaw's Friar's Head, a scenic, private golf course on Long Island. The difference is Ferry Point will be a daily fee course, whereas the cost to join Friar's Head is around $300,000. As of October 2003, Gagne said he and the rest of

Ferry Point's partners and the City of New York Parks and Recreation Department were still calculating green fee prices. City Parks and Ferry Point will team up to provide a tee time system that Gagne estimates will handle 50,000 rounds per year.

Prepare for a links-style layout, complete with wide fairways, and a small bucket of bump-and-run opportunities. Most of the holes overlook water—the 18th will be a memorable par-4 that will put players 300 feet from the East River's edge.

Other distinctions will make it special. The 12,000-square-foot clubhouse will be classic and rustic in design, but comfortable, and will go along with a waterfront restaurant and conference site to make a substantial complex. The overall condition of Ferry Point's layout will be maintained with the help of a state-of-the-art irrigation system.

Gagne is counting on a PGA Tour stop for his course by the 2008 season. The course is being built to host a regular season extravaganza, constructed with mounds for galleries and a huge parking lot. The location is superb. It's only a 20-minute drive from midtown Manhattan and even closer to LaGuardia International Airport.

"It's designed for the Tour," Gagne says. "It's a traditional Scottish course, but a player's course designed for high handicappers and challenging to all handicaps.

"Jack Nicklaus recognizes this as an extraordinary opportunity—300 acres of land this close to Manhattan is never going to be found again."

daytripper

So you want to test your ability somewhere else besides the lot of New York City courses. This someplace is less than two hours away and worth spending in the sunshine during your well-deserved day off.

You can't stray away too far. Remember that you're not collecting regular paychecks from the PGA Tour or LPGA circuit. You must be home early and well rested for the next day's workplace grind.

Just beyond the five boroughs, opportunities for public play are too numerous to mention. Long Island and West-chester alone possess enough day trip possibilities to satisfy a New York City player for a lifetime.

Plenty of road trip equations exist, whether they are in New York, New Jersey, or Connecticut. It's difficult for out-siders to comprehend how many quality courses are in the area. They're all waiting for your arrival. You simply have to know where the best fit is.

For city golfers, expanding their "must-play list" certainly is more expensive than a day at Silver Lake or Mosholu. There are higher green fees and higher costs for travel and food.

There are many, many opportunities for a higher reward for golfers who embrace new experiences. Don't forget a daytrip adventure is best when the regular foursome partakes.

Look for the course that best fits your: A) talents and B) desires. Call ahead and ask the attendants in the pro shop what to expect or talk with your local pro. He or she may have played the course and can suggest which tees to play and if it's going to be a day of target or links golf. If you don't like hitting a lot of iron shots off the tees (target golf) or you are opposed to playing in windy conditions (links golf) you may be disappointed with your daytrip.

Word of mouth is the most accurate compass to point you in the right direction. Golfing friends who either have played the course or who trust someone's knowledge—they've been there and done that—provide great tips. They're not invested in the course and can produce unbiased reviews.

With that said, trust me. I believe we've found enough excellent daytrip choices to pick from.

It wasn't easy at first, though.

After getting accustomed to life in the city, my next adjustment was locating golf courses in and around the city, including daytrips. One of my first daytrips was to The Links at Union Vale.

A memorable tale to say the least.

Just getting there gave me a sense of accomplishment. It meant two taxi rides and an hour or so train ride. Never did we travel to such extremes in South Carolina. The closest thing was a five-minute tram ride across the Intracoastal Waterway.

The daytrip started in Manhattan on Second Avenue with one hand clinging to the golf bag and the other signaling for a cab to go to Grand Central Station. By far, this was the easiest of all traveling transitions.

That soon changed. Once dropped off, I felt foolish with golf clubs strapped to my shoulders darting through morning rush hour into this colossal and historic Beaux Arts terminal. I may have well been naked standing in line to buy my train ticket. Any embarrassing thoughts, meanwhile, instantly faded away after I saw another person toting along clubs.

Once on board, my clubs occupied the seat next to me. No way was I going to store them above where they'd dangle overhead. I could picture the clubs falling onto someone's lap while at the same time a lawsuit dropped on mine. I figured if the train became too crowded that I could stand the clubs up between my legs. Sometimes comfort is overrated.

You'll be glad to know I didn't doze off as my stop came and went. All that remained was an innocent 15-minute taxi ride to the course.

But my taxi driver obviously didn't pass his Dutchess County 101 Tourism course. That made two of us. But a telephone call to the pro shop saved the day as well as my daytrip.

Nice course. Nice daytrip. Mark it down.

Maybe you're wondering about my trip home? It went fine. Well, OK, don't tell anyone, but my wife drove to Union Vale to pick me up.

Getting accustomed to living in the city has helped with my golf outside the city. Either by train or car, each daytrip becomes easier than the last.

Here are a handful of daytrip possibilities, either from past experiences the last few years or tips from golf writers in the metropolitan area. Take them for what they're worth.

But, I may boast, destination tips from golf writers are considered to be worth gold to any daytripper.

apple greens golf course

❖ *161 South Street*
Highland, NY 12528
845-883-5500
www.applegreens.com
Yardage: 6,576 (Championship markers); 6,080 (White);
5,356 (Gold); 4,959 (Forward).
Par: 71.
Architect: John Magaletta.

In 2003, Apple Greens harvested breathtaking views. This year will be more spectacular when its new crop is unveiled. Apple Greens' new nine literally will send golfers to greater heights and stunning views of the terrain, including Mohonk Towers. Substantial elevation changes are the norm for the course's newest addition, a unique back-to-back par-3 finish.

The original 18 is a solid course, but forgiving to all players. Once on course, players will find that Apple Greens lives up to its name. Apple trees are sprinkled throughout the layout and players are allowed to snack on apples all day.

The best time to play is in the fall when surrounding foliage is absolutely spectacular. And, play during the fall season isn't as hectic during summer months. Apple Greens is about two hours away from the Big Apple, but hasn't gone unnoticed. The new nine, meanwhile, should lessen the course's traffic.

And, Apple Greens' fees won't sour you on a potential visit. The cost on weekdays, including a cart, is less than $50. Players also have the option of walking Monday through Friday and on weekends and holidays after noon.

bethpage state park

❖ *Bethpage Parkway,*
Farmingdale, NY 11735
Main line: 516-249-0700
Access line: 516-249-0707
www.nysparks.state.ny.us
Black Course yardage: 7,299 (Championship markers);
6,655 (Middle); 6,119 (Forward).
Black Course par: 71.
Black Course architect: A.W. Tillinghast.
Blue Course yardage: 6,684 (Championship markers);
6,513 (Middle); 6,213 (Forward).
Blue Course par: 72.
Blue Course architect: A.W. Tillinghast.
Green Course yardage: 6,267 (Championship markers);
5,903 (Forward).
Green Course par: 71.
Green Course architect: Devereux Emmet, redesign by
A.W. Tillinghast.

Yellow Course yardage: 6,316 (Championship markers);
6,171 (Middle); 5,966 (Forward).

Yellow Course par: 71.

Yellow Course architect: Alfred Tull.

Red Course yardage: 6,875 (Championship markers);
6,537 (Middle); 6,198 (Forward).

Red Course par: 70.

Red Course architect: A.W. Tillinghast.

Play one round a year at the Black Course, site of the 2002 and 2009 U.S. Open, and your season is complete. Nowhere is there a course with major caliber conditions—Rees Jones gave it a facelift for the 2002 U.S. Open—that costs New York state residents less than $40 to play on weekdays. It's even a steal at double the cost for those non–New Yorkers lucky enough to get on.

The trick is getting on.

Seven days in advance you can try getting through the access telephone line; 16 lines open at 8:00 a.m., and any chance of landing a tee time is gone within three minutes. Everyone is allowed to make one phone reservation on the Black per month. Unfortunately for out-of-state residents, they must wait two days in advance before calling for a time.

There is another way. I'm familiar with it because I spent 15 hours in line to get on the Black.

The first hour of tee times on the Black is held for players who want to play so badly that they'll camp out in their cars in the Bethpage parking lot. There also is one foursome per hour held for those same brave souls.

Take it from Bethpage State Park director Dave Catalano that during the summer if you are not in the car line by Friday at 4:00 p.m., playing the Black anytime Saturday is doubtful. Weekdays are a bit easier: be there by 9:00 p.m. the night before and you should be fine. Unless the weather forecast is just short of a hurricane, walk-up times for the Black are usually sold out.

A word to the wise: don't camp out on Sundays because the Black is closed on Mondays. If you're camping out, get some sleep because you'll need the rest. The Black doesn't allow carts and it's an arduous walk—especially by the time you've started to climb to the 15th green.

But there are alternatives. Bethpage Black has four other quality courses, including the facility's most popular layout, the Red. The three "other" courses (Green, Blue, and Yellow) as well as the Red allow carts and cost less than the Black. Catalano says he believes more players prefer the Red because it's a superb layout that is extremely manageable for all levels of players.

Survivor: Bethpage Parking Lot

Camping out at the parking lot at Bethpage State Park consumes as much energy and strategic planning as waiting in line for New York Bruce Springsteen tickets.

The considerable amount of time spent in line? Suck it up and make the best of it.

Moreover, the wait is worth the effort. For first-timers the sensation is indescribable. The moment the starter bellows your group's name to hit away, you want to give him a hug and then run to the first tee.

Ready to go?

My first advice: Don't spend the night alone at Bethpage. It's boring, tiresome, and you don't know who you'll be paired with the next day. I'm all for making new friends, but when I devote 15 hours of my life to wait in a parking lot to play where Tiger Woods won a U.S. Open, it better be both pleasurable and memorable. I want to start the round with a snapshot of my regular foursome on the first tee that will forever be a reminder of playing the Black.

More importantly, being in a group means players can rotate time spent in the car until 4:30 to 5:00 a.m. when individuals have to be present. Eagle Scout certification isn't a qualification when camping out at Bethpage. No need to check your will. This golf experience won't kill you. But some, if not all of the following items will make an overnight stay at Bethpage State Park more comfortable.

*Shag bag full of range balls. There is a large enough grass area near the parking lot to work on your short game. This only works during daylight hours—not while it's pitch black, so to speak. At night you don't want to give the term "skull shot" new meaning to your partners.

*Deck of cards.

*Reading material such as your favorite golf book or golf magazine.

*Bethpage scorecard. Whether you're playing the Black, Red, Blue, Green, or Yellow, familiarize yourself with the course. It might be worth a shot or two.

*Flashlight for the deck of cards, favorite golf book, golf magazine, and Bethpage scorecard.

*Cooler filled with lunch and dinner and several bottles of water.

*Bethpage emergency kit: antacid tablets, toothbrush and toothpaste, mouthwash, bottle of the pink stuff, and aspirin.

*Extra change of clothes.

*Battery-operated radio. I'd rather use up two double-A batteries than the expensive energizer under the hood.

*Cell phone, to call loved ones or for an emergency. Call in a pizza delivery order. "I'm in the silver station wagon next to the red convertible in the Bethpage parking lot." Why not? But if you place this order, you'd better provide a bigger tip than usual.

*One of those Lone Ranger masks to cover your eyes. Between 2:30 and 4:00 a.m. car lights enter the parking lot frequently. You need at least a few hours of sleep to be able to hit a long drive on the Black's dog-leg right opening hole.

*Extra blanket. Even a summer night on Long Island requires a cover.

*Ear plugs. Sleeping in a car increases the odds that someone in your group (blush) will be an obnoxious snorer.

*An alarm, preferably a loud one. You don't want to wake up and watch all the cars cut in front.

*Golf hat in lieu of a brush or comb.

*Patience. Other than your golf clubs, golf shoes, and money to cover green fee, this is the most important item to pack.

bowling green golf course

❖ 53 Schoolhouse Road

Milton, NJ 07438

973-697-8688

www.bowlinggreengolf.com

Yardage: 6,811 (Championship markers); 6,450 (Blue); 6,045 (White); 5,763 (Yellow); 5,051 (Forward).

Par: 72.

Architect: Geoffrey Cornish.

This is truly a walker's paradise. Bowling Green's tall pines will remind you of courses in North Carolina without the high cost of Pinehurst. Out-of-town walking rates are in the $40 to $45 range Monday though Thursday.

Bowling Green was built in 1967 and features a memorable 600-yard finishing hole with the last 150 yards uphill. The Grille Room provides a good lunch, while you may want to dine at one of the Italian restaurants in Milton or Jefferson.

From Manhattan it's only an hour drive to the Carolinas, or in this case Bowling Green.

branton woods golf club

❖ *178 Stormville Road*
Hopewell Junction, NY 12533
845-223-1600
www.brantonwoodsgolf.com
Yardage: 7,100 (Championship markers); 6,817 (Blue); 6,329 (White); 5,837 (Gold); 4,857 (Forward).
Par: 72.
Architect: Eric Bergstol.

Unless you plan to invest in a membership, 2004 could be your last year to play Branton Woods. Owners of the 7,100-yard award-winning layout are planning on converting this to a private club in 2005. Branton Woods prides itself on championship conditions and the country club service within its magical Hudson Valley setting.

Monday through Thursday, New Yorkers can expect to pay $90 for green fee, which includes a cart and practice balls. Weekend rates increase to $135. There is a restaurant on site. But if you're already here you might as well go a few minutes out of the way to dine at Le Chambord, a five-star restaurant in Hopewell Junction.

centennial golf club

※ *185 John Simpson Road*
Carmel, NY 10512
845-225-5700

www.centennialgolf.com

Fairways/Meadows yardage: 7,050 (Championship markers); 6,538 (White); 5,841 (Gold); 5,208 (Forward).

Lakes/Fairways yardage: 7,133 (Championship markers); 6,614 (White); 5,900 (Gold); 5,208 (Forward).

Lakes/Meadows yardage: 7,115 (Championship markers); 6,524 (White); 5,859 (Gold); 5,208 (Forward).

Par: 72.

Architect: Larry Nelson.

Like Branton Woods, Centennial offers a private club setting that's open to the public. U.S. Open and two-time PGA Championship winner Larry Nelson designed this 27-hole gem. The nines on the Lakes and Meadows take players through plenty of elevation changes, while the Fairways nine is more of a traditional layout.

Centennial, open eight months out of the year, is about an hour drive north of Manhattan. Monday through Thursday expect to pay $95 including cart, while Friday through Sunday green fee and cart are $125.

crystal springs resort

※ *123 Crystal Springs Road*
Hamburg, NJ 07416
973-827-5996

www.crystalgolfresort.com

Ballyowen yardage: 7,094 (Championship markers); 6,508 (Blue); 6,066 (White); 5,531 (Gold); 4,903 (Forward).

Ballyowen par: 72.

Ballyowen architect: Roger Rulewich.

Black Bear yardage: 6,673 (Championship markers); 6,324 (Blue); 5,873 (White); 4,756 (Forward).

Black Bear par: 72.

Black Bear architects: David Glenz and Jack Kurlander.

Crystal Springs yardage: 6,808 (Championship markers); 6,361 (Blue); 5,874 (White); 5,111 (Forward).

Crystal Springs par: 72.

Crystal Springs architect: Robert Von Hagge.

The Spa yardage: 2,305 (Championship markers); 2,044 (Middle); 1,726 (Forward).

The Spa par: 31.

The Spa architect: Robert Trent Jones.

Wild Turkey yardage: 7,202 (Championship markers); 6,555 (Blue); 5,941 (White); 5,024 (Forward).

Wild Turkey par: 71.

Wild Turkey architect: Roger Rulewich.

Crystal Springs Resort is quickly becoming the star golfing attraction in New Jersey (with apologies to famed Pine Valley). Within its confines are five courses within five miles of each other, a massive clubhouse overlooking the Wild Turkey and Crystal Springs courses, and the Minerals center, which has 175 rooms, including suites and two presidential suites (check out weekend trips). The hotel is next to the Spa Golf Club, the Robert Trent Jones par-31 nine-hole layout.

All five courses are uniquely different from each other.

The Spa course is best for the beginner, while Black Bear, a player-friendly course, is a traditional 18-hole course with plenty of tree-lined fairways. Wild Turkey is the newest course with an eye-catching 208-yard par-3 over a quarry. Crystal Springs is target oriented. The course also has several challenging par-3s including the tenth, with an 80-foot drop off to an hourglass shaped green. The best and most expensive of the lot is Ballyowen Golf Club, considered by many to be New Jersey's finest public course. This is what a day in Scotland is like. The course is a links layout, with waist-high fescue and two-club winds. Crystal Springs' rates are somewhat expensive, but frequent golfer programs will make it affordable and well worth the miles.

lido golf club

❋ *255 Lido Boulevard*
Lido Beach, NY 11561
516-889-8181
www.Lidogolf.com
Yardage: 6,896 (Championship markers); 6,499 (Blue); 6,125 (White); 5,291 (Forward).
Par: 72.
Architect: Charles Blair Macdonald, redesign by Robert Trent Jones.

Chats with my father-in-law about New York golf courses usually include Long Island and its rich history. "Hey," roars the transplanted New Yorker, trying to get my attention, "when are you going to play Lido?"

That's a good question. The more I learn about Lido Golf Club, the more I want to take my 1-iron and smack my shin for not going.

There are plenty of reasons to go to a course that, before 1971, was off limits to the public.

The history and Lido Golf Club's two renowned architects are part of the draw: In 1914, Charles Blair Macdonald designed this original links masterpiece. During World War II, the Navy used the oceanside property. Robert Trent Jones was hired following the war to recreate Macdonald's work. According to Lido Golf Club's director of golf Steve Rofrano, Jones maintained "30 to 40 percent green-wise and tee wise to the way it was. He tried to keep the integrity intact."

There is the course: a true links challenge positioned between Reynolds Channel and the Atlantic Ocean with six holes nestled against the channel. I'd like for my father-in-law to join me on the famed par-5 16th "Channel Hole" to see if we both can survive back-to-back shots over water. We then could putt out on the original green designed by Macdonald.

An effortless journey: from Manhattan it's only a 25-minute Long Island Rail Road ride to Long Beach Station, plus a five-minute cab ride. Inexpensive to play: New Yorkers can walk the course any day of the week for less than $50.

Other activities: the beach is within walking distance and Long Beach has its share of restaurants, cafes, and bars.

Is there a reason not to go to Lido Golf Club?

Daytrips in the Boroughs

Memorable daytrips are in your backyard.

In other words, take advantage of being a tourist for a day within one of the five boroughs. Each has a multitude of attractions that stir both intellect and physical activity. Take, for example, golfers from Staten Island who dedicate a daytrip to the Bronx. Heaven forbid they learn something after touring their neighbors' neighborhoods.

Vice versa.

The same is true for residents in Queens and Brooklyn. And, though city players who reside in Manhattan don't have their own course, they can unfold their map and become a tourist in the four other boroughs. After all, we're one big family.

Daytrip possibilities in New York City are endless for couples, families, or regular foursomes who want to add to their day of golf.

Dining stops are necessary to fuel daytrips. Each borough boasts its culinary establishments are better than the other four. That's a buyer's market if there ever was one. City course regulars are happy to reveal their neighborhood's secret places to eat.

What are some borough possibilities?

In the Bronx, make a morning tee time at historic Van Cortlandt then take a short ride to either the Bronx Zoo or across the street to the New York Botanical Garden. You can also choose from the City Island fishing village restaurants or cheer on sports' most recognized organization at historic Yankee Stadium (tours are year-round).

On Staten Island, play La Tourette then venture off to the Gateway National Recreation Area (also in Brooklyn and Queens), Historic Richmond Town, the Snug Harbour Cultural Center, the Botanical Garden featuring the New York Chinese Scholar's Garden, or bring a baseball glove to snag foul balls at Richmond County Bank Ballpark where the Staten Island Yankees play.

A perfect summer day in Brooklyn might be to tee it up at Marine Park then ride the Wonder Wheel at Coney Island, grab a hotdog at Nathan's, take a stroll on the boardwalk, and finish the day at Keyspan Park to watch the New York Mets minor league team, the Brooklyn Cyclones. Other prominent Brooklyn attractions are its Botanical Garden, New York Aquarium, Academy of Music, and Children's Museum, one of the oldest in the United States.

After a round at Douglaston, city golfers can become spectators in Queens; they can see horse racing at Aqueduct or Belmont Park, Mets baseball at Shea Stadium, and in late August/early September, the U.S. Open at the National Tennis Center. Queens also welcomes visitors to its newly opened Louis Armstrong House, Museum for African Art, P.S.1 Contemporary

Art Center, Botanical Garden, and for the silver screen buffs, the American Museum of the Moving Image.

Manhattan's daytrip possibilities are endless. Work on your short game at either Chelsea Piers or Randalls Island, and then relax at Central Park and visit its zoo; go to Times Square to sightsee; catch a show on Broadway or at Harlem's Apollo Theater; stroll along Museum Mile on Fifth Avenue; or go downtown to shop and dine at the South Street Seaport.

patriot hills golf club

❋ *19 Clubhouse Lane*
Stony Point, NY 10908
845-947-7085
www.patriothillsgolfclub.com
Yardage: 6,502 (Championship markers); 6,119 (Middle);
5,629 (White); 5,101 (Forward).
Par: 71.
Architect: Rick Jacobson.

The layout at Patriot Hills is perhaps the closest country setting to New York City. Minutes off the Palisades Parkway lies the one-year-old course and its stunning mountain views.

A couple holes are within view of the Hudson River, while a breathtaking elevation change stops players in their non-metal spikes. Three par-3s are practically on mountains, making this course impossible to travel by foot. The 467-yard par-4 4th also is one of Patriot Hills' most memorable holes.

Patriot Hills is more player-friendly following 2003's debut season. Players now are allowed to stray off cart paths, which is sure to improve the pace of play issues. The facility's restaurant will offer ballroom seating for up to 500 guests.

Regular rates are $85 during weekdays and $120 on weekends. Keep in mind rates at Patriot Hills will vary. Twilight rates (after 2:00 p.m.) and super twilight rates (after 4:00 p.m.) are more affordable.

royce brook golf club

※ *201 Hamilton Road*
Hillsborough, NJ 08844
888-434-3673
www.roycebrook.com
East yardage: 6,946 (Championship markers); 6,997 (Green); 5,935 (White); 5,014 (Forward).
East par: 72.
East architect: Steve Smyers.

The folks at Royce Brook do their best to showcase a country club atmosphere where even forecaddies ($10 per player not including gratuity) are mandatory from June to August.

This may be the closest a municipal player can get to a private facility. Literally. Royce Brook has two worthwhile courses, but only the East is open to the public. The West course went private in December of 2002. But, there is an option to play the West through its corporate portfolio program, allowing players to become a "member" for a day.

By no means does the East course drop off in design or conditions. Players intimidated by forced carries will especially enjoy playing the East—the course has zero forced carries. It's open year-round and costs New Yorkers just less than $100 on weekdays. Royce Brook also has an accommodation package with the Double Tree Hotel, located 12 minutes from the two courses.

the golf club at mansion ridge

❋ *1292 Orange Turnpike*
Monroe, NY 10950

845-782-7888

www.mansionridgegolf.com

Yardage: 6,889 (Tour markers); 6,462 (Championship);
6,134 (Players); 5,697 (Resort); 4,785 (Forward).

Par: 72.

Architect: Jack Nicklaus.

The Golf Club at Mansion Ridge is a popular pilgrimage for city dwellers. The much-traveled path from New York City to the Hudson Valley course began in 1999 when the Jack Nicklaus–signature design opened its undulating greens.

This design is still unique to our area. It's the course Jack built, his first New York public course. The Golden Bear factor overshadows the course's pricey green fees. Visitors can expect to pay around $90 Monday through Thursday and more than $130 on the weekends.

Joe Pesci and Adam Sandler left their acting careers behind for a day with intentions to be stars on the difficult par-5 ninth and its two forced carries over water. New York legends Lawrence Taylor and Roger Clemens have been seen sporting around the 6,889-yard course.

It's as big a hit for visiting golfers, just as the nearby upscale outlet center, Woodbury Commons, is a magnet for avid shoppers. A trip to Mansion Ridge puts in you close range to West Point, the nation's oldest military academy, and Bear Mountain State Park and Bear Mountain Inn. Picnic areas, a swimming pool, natural trails, boat rental, fishing, and a zoo attract park visitors.

The alluring quality about Mansion Ridge is you don't have to play like Jack Nicklaus to have fun on the course. Players can pick from one of five tee settings, from the 6,889-yard championship tees to 4,785-yard forward markers.

tallgrass golf club

✳ *24 Cooper Street*
Shoreham, NY 11786
631-209-9359
www.tallgrassgolf.com
Yardage: 6,587 (Championship markers); 6,148 (Blue);
5,613 (White); 5,044 (Forward).
Par: 71.
Architect: Gil Hanse.

Links courses in the heart of Long Island are difficult to get on. Here's an exception to the Long Island rule. The driving distance to Tallgrass Golf Club near the north shore may stretch your day, but it's worth the long haul. Weekday rates for New York City residents are just less than $80 on weekdays and $90 on weekends. Players can take the Long Island Rail Road stop to the Port Jefferson station, followed by a 15-minute cab ride to the course.

Winds slightly tilt your hat as you proceed from the parking lot to the clubhouse, your first sign a day of links golf is ahead. A good mix of difficult and relatively easy par-4s and par-3s along with constant winds force players to use most, if not all their clubs.

The course's name doesn't mean your long-iron game will be tangled in tall grass all day. Tallgrass is short by today's standards (6,587 yards from the championship markers), and the widths of its fairways are player friendly.

the links at union vale

❖ *153 North Parliman Road*
Union Vale, NY 12540
845-223-1000
www.thelinksatunionvale.com
Yardage: 6,954 (Championship markers); 6,646 (Middle);
6,216 (Middle); 5,198 (Forward).
Par: 72.
Architect: Stephen Kay.

Ireland isn't as far away as you thought. Just go to The Links at Union Vale where you swear you are in the country instead of Dutchess County.

A few years ago a group of Irish Americans who reside in the city opened this links style course on farmland in Dutchess County. It's open to the public, but The Links at Union Vale has more than 450 equity members, 90 percent of whom are Irish born.

Oddly enough, some of its members have never stepped foot on the course. They joined simply out of pride for their old country, wanting to be a part of an Irish club that's an hour-and-half north of New York City. Even the course professional speaks with a brogue.

The Links at Union Vale favors the stronger player who can handle two 600-yard par-5s, pesky winds, and tall rough that cruelly snags both clubfaces and golf balls. Course officials have taken note of the high rough and plan on trimming the grass to manageable heights.

As in Ireland, players are encouraged to walk The Links at Union Vale. New Yorkers can walk the course on weekdays for less than $50 and on weekends for less than $70. And, also as in the Emerald Isle, the 19th hole is as lively as a Dublin pub.

the course at yale

✳ *Conrad Drive*
New Haven, CT 06520
203-392-2380
Yardage: 6,749 (Championship markers); 6,440 (Middle);
5,941 (Middle); 5,209 (Forward).
Par: 70.
Architect: Charles Blair Macdonald.

The Course at Yale destination is as unique as it is fascinating.

By design it's fascinating. It's unique because during most of the season the Yale Course is a private facility.

The operative word being "most" of the season.

In order to get on the venerable course, most of the time you have to be introduced if not accompanied by a member at $120 per pop. But there is a window for public play on the historic Charles Blair Macdonald course located ten minutes from campus.

During the fall months, the course is open to the public. The Yale public special is $75 for green fee, cart, and lunch. Make sure to call the pro shop to find out when the fall special runs.

It's only been a few years since the Yale Course introduced its special public play policy. Avid golfers value a day on this demanding course with its variety of hilly conditions and blind shots as an opportunity of a lifetime.

Definitely, the Yale Course, restored and updated in 2003 by Roger Rulewich, is considered one of the true architectural gems. It's worth a two-hour drive from New York City or a Metro North train ride.

Daytrip Helper

www.nygolfshuttle.com

718-740-6657

This group makes getting on course sound too easy. Easy but expensive.

NYGolfShuttle can arrange tee times at some of the metropolitan area's favorite golf stops with transportation included.

This service takes away the risk of an aching bad back from camping out in the car while waiting in line to play Bethpage Black. This way, players have NYGolfShuttle make a time for a single, twosome, threesome, or foursome to get on the 2002, 2009 U.S. Open course. Golfers are chauffeured roundtrip by a limousine.

Of course, the price is just a tad higher than the $31 weekday rate a New Yorker dished out to play the Black in 2003. The cost for the Bethpage trip is $400 per player for a foursome and as high as $500 to sign up as a single.

All five Bethpage courses are part of NYGolfShuttle package deals, as well as Montauk Downs ($400 per player in a foursome only), Ballyowen ($300), Centennial ($250), Royce Brook ($250), and New York City municipal courses Douglaston ($100) and Clearview ($100).

About 90 percent of the people who use golf's travel version for the rich and famous opt for Bethpage Black. But the ideal package is Montauk Downs, considering rising gas prices and traffic headaches encountered en route to the eastern tip of Long Island. Driving through the Hamptons can't be any simpler.

extended trips

Daytrips are good for getting away. But they can fall short of satisfying a golfer's passion to truly escape New York City's hustle and bustle lifestyle.

It's possible for a daytrip experience, if not planned well, to be chaotic. You're in such a mad rush to beat the traffic—or wrong directions take you to the wrong exit—that once you get to the first tee you're already worn out. If you don't play well you remember more about the lofty digits on the score-card than the overall experience. And, you're either too wired or exhausted to reminisce as the pillow cradles your head.

In other words, you need a day off to recoup from your day off.

There is a cure-all. It's the extended version of the daytrip. Everyone should have in his or her working contract a clause providing a three-day golf pass.

There should be such a bill presented before Congress. Yes, it should be a law.

Everyone under this umbrella would prosper.

The working environment would get happier, healthier, and more productive employees. Each employee would have an improved short-game touch and a lower handicap. And, golf courses and their respective communities would receive a significant economic boon.

New York City residents are especially in need of such a reform in the workplace. Many struggle with major workloads, begrudgingly carrying laptops home and dreaming about work-related problems in their sleep. Today's popular expression "24/7" underscores the seriousness with which New Yorkers take their careers.

Sometimes they need more than a one-day break.

Three-day and two-day golf packages are popular get-aways. Resorts that meet your needs are either an hour's drive or three or four hours away. If it's the latter, try to get away Thursday instead of Friday because of likely traffic headaches.

With one exception, the following golf destinations are located outside the New York City daytrip zip codes. Most are resort-oriented destinations and are known for their gorgeous layouts, especially tempting to golfers.

These selections have different costs, different driving distances from New York City, and different activities other than golf. Some are made to spend the entire time on the resort property. Others are known for tourist stops along the way or in the neighborhood.

Of course, there are more than these possibilities for New York residents to choose from.

Each synopsis can help you determine which extended getaway fits your golfing passions. While some literally wine and dine their guests, other golfing outlets rely strictly on a total golf experience—fancy frills are not offered nor are they requested.

Wherever you choose, allow resorts to pamper you, from the pro shop staff to the concierge. Their goal is to seduce the weekend vacationer, to make them fall in love with the resort for return visits.

So let the resort do all the work. Somebody has to.

concord resort & golf club/grossinger country club

✴ *Concord Resort*
Kiamesha Lake, NY 12751
845-794-4000
www.concordresort.com
Monster Course yardage: 7,650 (Championship markers); 7,471 (Blue); 6,989 (White); 6,548 (Red); 5,201 (Forward).
Monster Course par: 72.
Monster Course architect: Joseph Finger.
International Course yardage: 6,619 (Championship

markers); 5,968 (Middle); 5,554 (Forward).

International Course par: 71.

International architect: Alfred H. Tull.

❖ *Grossinger Country Club*
26 Route 52 East
Liberty, NY 12754
845-292-9000

Big G Course yardage: 6,907 (Championship); 6,456 (Middle); 5,730 (Forward).

Big G Course par: 71.

Big G architect: A.W. Tillinghast, redesign by Joseph Finger.

Little G Course yardage: 3,268 (Championship markers); 3,166 (Middle); 3,024 (Forward).

Little G Course par: 36.

Little G Course architect: A.W. Tillinghast.

While the Concord Resort & Golf Club and Grossinger Country Club are not your mom or dad's weekend destination, the golf at both is worth the 90-minute drive.

At one time they were known for their full resort packages, including live entertainment. Until the resort owners give the go ahead to begin a major new project—not likely for five years according to a Concord representative—New Yorkers have an opportunity to use this as a frequent golfing paradise. Soon green fees will increase when construction begins on the "new" resort.

A combined 63 holes, the Concord Golf Club and Grossinger are open from April until the beginning of November. During summer, there is an unlimited golf package for $395 per person, which also includes two nights' accommodations, range balls, two breakfasts, a fruit basket, club cleaning and storage, and pro shop discounts.

The same package from April to mid-May and from October through the end of the season is $310 per person.

Players stay in one of 42 rooms at the Concord. Overbooking is never a problem. In the past, Concord officials have arranged alternative lodging for their guests to stay in while providing the same on-course privileges. The rooms aren't "four-star" quality, but are plenty comfortable for guests worn out after trying to tame the "Monster."

The Monster, a lengthy layout designed in 1964 by Joseph Finger with help from legendary pros Jimmy Demaret and Jackie Burke, Jr., has a monstrous reputation. Legendary Gene Sarazen, champion of all four majors, walked off the last green and described the course as a "damn monster." Sarazen also told the owner never to change a blade of grass on the course because it's perfect.

Sarazen's playful moniker stuck. Truly a monster, the course can be stretched more than 7,600 yards from the championship markers. How many courses can you name that play 7,400 yards from non-championship tees?

Concord's International course, built in 1950, is more forgiving than its sister course. The Alfred H. Tull design plays a maximum of 6,619 yards.

Located 12 miles from Concord, Grossinger in Liberty has two courses designed by famed architect A.W. Tillinghast.

The "Big G" course is easier on the ego than the Monster, but matches it in tradition. The Big G and its island green par-5 played host to the New York Open from 1978 to 1988. During a poll taken by golfers in surrounding counties, Grossinger was labeled the best course in the region, followed by the Monster course and Mansion Ridge.

Although it's only nine holes, the ``Little G" is a par-36 course that is just as demanding and fun as its big brother.

conklin players club

✳ *1520 Conklin Road*
Conklin, NY 13748
607-775-3042
www.conklinplayers.com
Yardage: 6,772 (Championship markers); 6,128 (White);
5,568 (Gold); 4,699 (Forward).
Par: 72.
Architect: Rick Rickard.

You may complain about the three-hour drive, but this lengthy highway excursion is a path to a little bit of everything. This is wine country, so prepare your palate. Two shopping malls and the Ross Park Zoo provide golfers and families with enough alternatives away from the fairways.

Besides its 6,772-yard par-72 layout, the Conklin Players Club trip includes reasonable package deals with accommodations and golf at the Heritage Club, the Links at Hiawatha Landing, and at En-Joie Golf Course, a PGA Tour stop. All four courses are located within a 20-mile radius of each other.

Conklin has a two-day weekend package for around $200 with two rounds of golf, one night's lodging, breakfast, lunch each day at the course, and range balls. Because few holes require forced carries, Conklin Players Club attracts more women players than most resorts.

Players have the option of staying at the Regency, Holiday Inn, Sheraton, or several other hotels.

Conklin officials claim they're a magnet for weekend visitors from New York City, Syracuse, and Albany.

Guests need only call a few days in advance to secure reservations. April is a more flexible period, while Conklin's peak time is June through September. Lower rates are available in October and April. Course officials brag that their fairways are plush from the beginning of the season until the end.

Conklin Players Club is open from April through October.

crystal springs resort

❊ *123 Crystal Springs Road*
Hamburg, NJ 07416

973-827-5996

www.crystalgolfresort.com

Ballyowen yardage: 7,094 (Championship markers); 6,508 (Blue); 6,066 (White); 5,531 (Gold); 4,903 (Forward).

Ballyowen par: 72.

Ballyowen architect: Roger Rulewich.

Black Bear yardage: 6,673 (Championship markers); 6,324 (Blue); 5,873 (White); 4,756 (Forward).

Black Bear par: 72.

Black Bear architects: David Glenz and Jack Kurlander.

Crystal Springs yardage: 6,808 (Championship markers); 6,361 (Blue); 5,874 (White); 5,111 (Forward).

Crystal Springs par: 72.

Crystal Springs architect: Robert Von Hagge.

The Spa yardage: 2,305 (Championship markers); 2,044 (Middle); 1,726 (Forward).

The Spa par: 31.

The Spa architect: Robert Trent Jones.

Wild Turkey yardage: 7,202 (Championship markers); 6,555 (Blue); 5,941 (White); 5,024 (Forward).

Wild Turkey par: 71.

Wild Turkey architect: Roger Rulewich.

This isn't a duplication error. Crystal Springs did appear in our section on daytrips. The always-expanding resort is also ideal for city residents to use as a weekend getaway.

Five courses—including Robert Trent Jones' nine-hole layout—are an hour and a half drive from the George Washington Bridge to lure links enthusiasts. And, two more courses are on the Crystal Springs Resort blueprints. Architect Roger Rulewich, who designed both Wild Turkey and the classic heathland-style Ballyowen, was scheduled to break ground on the resort's sixth course in the spring of 2004 with completion anticipated for 2005.

David Glenz, the 1998 national PGA Teacher of the year and nine-time New Jersey instructor of the year, has an on-site academy with various curriculums. Glenz has three- and one-day programs and half-day short game and full-swing classes.

Four of the five courses usually remain open from mid-March through mid-December. Black Bear is kept open year-round, pending Old Man Winter and Jack Frost.

But Crystal Springs Resort offers more than simply golf, golf, golf. True, it's located in the middle of Nowhere, New Jersey, but the resort is a massive playground for weekend visitors. Metropolitan area players may consider this golf's version of Disney World.

Minerals, a 175-room deluxe accommodation facility, is one of three new additions. It opened in the fall of 2003, and overnight rates range from $150 to $225. Big spenders likely will want to inquire about Minerals' upgrades, possibly to either one of the two presidential suites.

The Elements and Minerals Sports Clubs were designed with the weekender in mind. Elements is a relaxing place to receive a full spa treatment, while Minerals Sports Club has a state-of-the-art workout center with cardiovascular machines and personal trainers.

If you or your family can't find enough to do within the confines of Crystal Springs, there is nearby Mountain Creek with outdoor activities in the summer and winter. The area is conducive to antiquing, apple and pumpkin pickin', horse-back riding, and plenty of shopping.

en-joie golf course

✤ *722 West Main Street*
Endicott, NY 13760

888-436-5643

www.enjoiegolf.com

Yardage: 7,034 (Championship markers); 6,680 (Middle);
6,249 (Middle); 5,477 (Front).

Par: 72.

Architect: Ernie Smith, redesign by Michael Hurdzan.

Play a municipal course where PGA Tour swingers tee it up.
This isn't a story about getting on Bethpage Black, but taking
aim at the annual PGA Tour site for the B.C. Open.

It's such an affordable deal that it's inconceivable in this
day of triple-digit green fees. Sure, En-Joie Golf Course is
nearly a four-hour haul, but it's well worth the $50 weekend
rates (with cart) and $38 rates on weekdays. Locals say find-
ing overnight accommodations near the course is never a
problem. Rates start at $45 per night.

En-Joie is one of only three regular PGA Tour stops
played on a municipal course. The best time to schedule a
trip here is during June, when the course is in condition for
the world's best golfers.

Even if green fees were considerably higher, En-Joie
would continue to attract players to its fairways.

The course is adorned with defined tree lines and has very
little undulation. In the late 1990s architect Michael Hurdzan was
brought in to do $3.5 million in major renovations. En-Joie's sig-
nature test is the long par-4 15th. Year-in and year-out the PGA
Tour rates it as one of the toughest holes in the United States.

During the B.C. Open, you'll want to check with course
operations to find out when the course is closing and reopen-
ing. The year 2004 marks the 33rd B.C. Open, and if you're in
the neighborhood during tourney week, call the tournament
office (607-754-2482) about tickets to the event.

Last year, Craig Stadler was the surprise B.C. Open winner, becoming the first 50-and-over player to record victories in the same season on both the PGA Tour and Champions Tour. Amateurs who play En-Joie will be walking in the footsteps of past B.C. Open champions Brad Faxon, 2004 U.S. Ryder Cup captain Hal Sutton, John Daly, Fred Couples, and Tom Kite.

There is plenty of outdoor activity in this part of the Finger Lakes region, adjacent to Seneca and Cayuga Lakes.

Plane gliding is popular, and balloon races soar especially high in August. For those who'd prefer keeping their feet on ground, there are shopping plazas, the Corning Glass Works, and several parks in the vicinity. Small concerts in the summer are always playing within hearing distance.

the links at hiawatha landing

✣ *2350 Marshland Road*
Apalachin, NY 13732
607-687-6952
www.hiawathalinks.com
Yardage: 7,104 (Championship markers); 6,586 (Blue); 6,195 (White); 5,801 (Green); 5,101 (Forward).
Par: 72.
Architects: Brian Silva and Mike Mungeam.

In the middle of January the telephone at the Links at Hiawatha Landing starts ringing for reservations. Callers are getting an early jump on a course that doesn't usually open until mid-March.

Hiawatha Landing is a links style course, different from the Conklin Players Club and the Heritage, with which it shares package-play opportunities.

The course is a typical links layout, with two- to three-foot tall fescue rough and 20-mile-per-hour winds. High handicappers are relieved to find out Hiawatha Landing offers five sets of tees and zero gimmick holes.

Looking for a good deal? Stay two weekday nights, play three rounds of golf, and receive two breakfasts all for $145. The weekend package is the same itinerary but costs $285. Daily rates range in the mid-$60s on weekends and mid-$40s on weekdays.

Apalachin is a peaceful community, but with plenty of chances to stay busy. One course representatives says it's "a little city without the congestion." It's known for its antiquing, shopping malls, and popular dining spots. There is a winery 40 minutes away.

montauk downs state park

❖ *South Fairview Avenue*
Montauk, NY 11954
Clubhouse: 631-668-1100
Tee time access: 631-668-5000
Yardage: 6,762 (Championship markers); 6,289 (Middle);
5,797 (Forward).
Par: 72.
Architect: Robert Trent Jones.

Montauk Downs State Park is eastern Long Island's answer to Bethpage Black.

The New York State Department of Parks and Recreation operates both. Both are affordable. Both tempt players to the point they'll camp out the night before in the parking lot. And, both can be notoriously taxing to the scorecard.

Upon arrival at the Robert Trent Jones course—the famed architect did a complete makeover in 1968—you may hear that Montauk Downs is tougher than its sister course in Farmingdale. The 2002 U.S. Open course is longer, but constant stronger gusts at Montauk Downs may even the score.

A links layout, every hole at Montauk Downs is affected by gusts from the Atlantic Ocean. At the least, count on ten-mile-per-hour winds interfering with thoughts about your swing.

This is both for the serious and casual New York City golfer. Sure, Montauk's cozy setting and signature lighthouse at the end of the island make it a tourist haven. Plenty of mom and pop hotels in the area, too.

But whatever time Friday you begin the Montauk trek on the Long Island Expressway, a two-hour-plus drive easily can turn into a four-hour pain in the hosel. Every Montauk-bound foursome should arrive on site with tee times already booked.

Operating on a similar telephone reservation system as the Black, Montauk Down's weekend tee times expire almost as quickly. The morning's first six times are allotted to players who wait in line. Two foursomes per hour are also open for "walk-up" players.

On a typical August weekend, regulars are in line by 3:00 a.m. But the quantity is smaller than up the road at Bethpage's multi-complex facility.

Sometimes, there are Sunday afternoon openings. That's when the majority of "locals" depart to their primary residence.

Montauk Downs is always busy because it's thought of as one of the best public golf courses in the United States. In-state residents can't beat the price: $30 on weekdays and $36 on weekends. Green fees double for those with a license outside of New York state.

new jersey national golf club

❋ *579 Allen Road*
Basking Ridge, NJ 07920
908-781-9400
www.newjerseynational.com
Yardage: 7,056 (Championship markers); 6,725 (Blue);

6,373 (White); 5,636 (Gold); 5,019 (Forward).

Par: 72.

Architect: Roy Case.

Fifty minutes is all it takes to transport yourself from the city's fast paced lifestyle to the country setting of New Jersey National Golf Club. The semi-private course, built in 1996, is blessed with a soothing tree-lined sanctuary where each hole is distinctively different.

But public play opportunities soon will come to an end. When New Jersey National reaches 200 members it will become fully private. Until then, course officials are expecting public play in 2004. Players can call for times six days in advance.

Closed the first two months of the year, New Jersey National is lethal in difficulty but picturesque in design.

Every caliber of player is suited for New Jersey National's wide, rolling fairways, undulating greens, and "country club" conditions. An inordinate number of tee markers—four for men and two for women—provide players with more than enough options.

New Yorkers should consider a July or August excursion. Expect to pay $150 and $90 for weekend and weekday rates, respectively. There is a twilight discount (after 4:00 p.m.) for which guests dish out $80 on weekends and $60 on weekdays.

The closest overnight accommodation is within minutes of the course, the Somerset Hills Hotel. The area offers fine dining at the Three West restaurant, and there are outlet centers within three miles. Trails for horseback riding and biking and facilities for sharpshooters to hone their skeet-shooting eyes are in the area.

nevele grande resort & country club

❊ *Ellenville, NY 12428*

800-647-6000

www.nevele.com

Blue/Red Course yardage: 6,823 (Championship markers); 6,223 (Middle); 5,736 (Middle); 5,145 (Front).

Blue/Red par: 70.

Red/White yardage: 6,532 (Championship markers); 5,889 (Middle); 4,570 (Front).

Red/White par: 70.

White/Blue yardage: 6,573 (Championship markers); 6,012 (Middle); 5,613 (Front).

White/Blue par: 70.

Architect: Robert Trent Jones, redesign by Tom Fazio.

Anywhere that has the work of both Robert Trent Jones and Tom Fazio should instantly lure golfers. This particular anywhere is a 27-hole facility within the comfortable confines of the Catskills, an hour-and-a-half away from New York City.

With a patriotic flair, the nine-hole courses are dubbed Red, White, and Blue. Fazio redesigned the Red and White, each course guiding players along and over finger lakes. Jones did the Blue, the longest of the three.

Nevele Grande is a massive 800-acre playground. A $10 million renovation project gave it more than simply a typical facelift. It's a getaway where adults can turn back the clock and be kids again.

Besides golf, guests have many athletic activities to pick from. They would need more than a week to enjoy everything Nevele Grande has to offer.

For starters, there is a new fitness center. Tennis, anyone? You can play on any one of 15 all-weather tennis courts (five with lights) or 12 indoor tennis courts. There also are four racquetball courts; five pools, including an Olympic size and a diving pool; horseback riding; roller blading; volleyball; shuffleboard; badminton; basketball; and softball. Fishing, too, is available. Guests, provided they are carrying a New York state fishing license, can cast for trout, pickerel, and bass.

Winter enthusiasts are not overlooked. Nevele Grande is a popular destination for ice-skating, skiing, snow tubing, and cross-country skiing.

There is enough room for your foursome, your friend's foursome, and a friend of your friend's foursome. A 700-room facility handles plenty of activity, including nightly live entertainment—usually a comedian or singer—in the Stardust Room.

The ballpark figure for weekend golf packages (two days of golf) is around $250 per room each night. Prices are less on weekdays. Kids 16 and under stay free.

Inquire about special packages throughout the year.

seaview marriott bay and pine courses

❖ *401 South New York Road*
Absecon, N.J. 08205
609-748-7680
www.seaviewgolf.com
Bay Course yardage: 6,247 (Championship markers);
6,011 (Middle); 5,017 (Forward).
Bay Course par: 71.
Bay Course architect: Donald Ross, redesign by A.W. Tillinghast.
Pine Course yardage: 6,731 (Championship markers);
6,211 (Middle); 5,216 (Forward).
Pine Course par: 71.
Pine Course architects: William S. Flynn and Howard Toomey, redesign by Bob Copp, Jr.

The Bay and Pine courses are two of the old guards. In fact, one of the two is celebrating its 90th birthday in 2004.

Arguably the Bay is the most recognized. Designed in 1914 by Donald Ross, the Bay is the host site each June to the LPGA ShopRite Classic. It's a links-style course incorporating Ross's signatures, especially crowned greens similar to Pinehurst No. 2.

On the Bay, players enjoy face-to-face encounters with gently rolling fairways and panoramic views of the ocean and the Atlantic City skyline.

In 1942, Sam Snead won his first professional major at the Bay Course, [defeating Jim Turnesa 2 and 1] in the PGA Championship.

The Pine Course may be younger—it opened in 1929—but is longer than its sister course. Each hole is considered to possess "private club" qualities. Most holes are so distinctively bordered by woods that players may feel they have the whole course to themselves.

Golfers can strategize their weekend at the Seaview Marriott, a four-diamond resort.

One trend is for players to arrive by mid-afternoon to play one of the courses at a special $59 twilight rate. Saturday and Sunday morning green fees are $129, while rooms are $200 and higher, varying on demand.

The Nick Faldo Golf Institute is onsite for golfers who can't swing enough. Players can use the outdoor or year-round indoor facilities. There is also a one-hour complimentary clinic each day.

Too much golf? Ease shoulder pains by getting a massage on site at the Elizabeth Arden Red Door Spa. The beach and Atlantic City are short drives away. Notwithstanding its two golf courses, Seaview is best known for exposing its guests to culinary delights. Chef Jim Tripi is listed as one of the Marriott's top ten chefs. His seafood buffets (May through November) and Sunday brunches are extremely popular.

twisted dune golf club

✻ *2101 Ocean Heights Avenue*
Egg Harbor Township, NJ 08234
609-653-8019
Yardage: 7,283 (Championship markers); 6,681 (Middle);
5,617 (Forward).
Par: 72.
Architect: Archie Struthers.

The moniker Twisted Dune is a helpful description of what kind of golf course you're in store for: a links layout capable of tying you in a knot.

The Scottish-style course is easier than it registers on the scorecard, thanks to wide fairways and a fairly forgiving first cut of rough. But stay out of the course's cumbersome fescue.

It's a layout that has received many accolades from major golf publications. Twisted Dune's impeccable playing conditions add to its shank-proof reputation. And, the practice area is popular because of its full turf driving range and short-game area.

Twisted Dune offers package deals with approximately a dozen hotels in the area. Green fees vary from $49 to $99, based on the season and the day of the week.

Once the round is completed, join the family for a 15-minute drive to historic Smithville or a 25-minute ride to Cape May, the southernmost point of New Jersey. Both stops have craft shops, while at Cape May you can make dinner plans for an evening overlooking the Atlantic Ocean.

dream on

Ever sit back and daydream about the best courses you've played?

Ever sit back and daydream about the best courses you haven't played?

My answers are "yes" and "yes."

If I died today my collection of logo balls—purchased only from courses I've played—would be, well, rated outstanding.

It's not ironic that three of the five dream stops were in the metropolitan area. New Yorkers, go ahead and boast. This area has some of the world's most cherished golf courses.

Not many will argue. They can't.

Thank you, Long Island.

Thank you, Westchester.

Thank you, New Jersey.

And, thank you, Connecticut.

My all-time five favorites played are the Augusta National Golf Club; The K Club outside Dublin, Ireland; Shinnecock Hills Golf Club; Bethpage Black; and Winged Foot's West Course.

Although other elite, tradition-rich courses are within the area, I can't foresee replacing anytime soon the aforementioned five.

As if the experiences happened less than a second ago, I recollect severe first-tee jitters. There particularly were problems with Mr. Woods—I'm not referring to Tiger, either.

At Augusta—three alarms were set so as not to oversleep—I started on the tenth, and from the members' tee I blasted a 3-wood through the fairway and into the woods. At the K Club, I pulled my first shot into the woods. On the Black, I faded my opening tee shot behind a tree.

My luck changed at Shinnecock—I splashed one in the right bunker. Fortunately, at Winged Foot I found the middle of the fairway.

Everyone has his or her way of determining a dream course.

Tradition usually is the number one factor. Is this the place where Ben Hogan perfectly framed his patented picture-perfect follow-through, or where Byron Nelson recorded one of a record 11 consecutive victories? Does this place have the finishing hole where Corey Pavin recorded one of the U.S. Open's most miraculous shots, or the green on which Justin Leonard drained the longest of putts to secure a U.S. victory in the Ryder Cup?

Moreover, have majors been held on your dream courses? If so, how many U.S. Opens, British Opens, or PGA Championships?

Did yesteryear's architects A.W. Tillinghast, Donald Ross, Charles Blair Macdonald, Seth Raynor, or Robert Trent Jones come up with the course's blueprints? Or are your dream courses designed by some of today's architectural masterminds: Pete Dye, Rees Jones, Tom Fazio, or Jack Nicklaus?

Dream courses can be new, bold layouts. It didn't take long for Bandon Dunes' two courses to become a pair of the most sought-after courses on golfers' must-play lists. Rare new green jewels are rampantly coveted in the players' market. Not many have played them, but everyone wants to.

Is your dream course recognized for a mouth-watering signature stretch or one particular hole? Such signatures have the ability to provide nightmares and at the same time a vision of unmatched beauty. Dream destinations have an Amen Corner, Road Hole, Blue Monster, or the 17th island green at the Tournament Players Club Stadium course.

Unforgettable home holes complete the dream. Pebble Beach's 18th, with players firing tee shots over waves crashing into the shoreline. Harbour Town Golf Links' 18th, where views of the Calibogue Sound and the lighthouse are forever fixtures in our memories. The Old Course at St. Andrews and its short par-4 and Valley of Sin, with onlookers peering from the Royal & Ancient clubhouse and other venerable buildings.

Your dream selection may include one or more of those tradition-rich "major" courses, famed architects, world-famous signature stretches, or fantastic home holes.

Maybe your criteria call for something altogether different.

Golf gives us innumerable quality courses throughout the world. That number continues to grow.

That's what makes the sport so appealing: it's universal. Every state can claim it has one dream course. Ask golfers from Alabama to Wyoming, and they'll quickly identify their state's golfing paradise.

Probably every country can claim a dream course. Bet you didn't know Estonia has a golf course.

We may not have heard about it, but every golfer embraces his or her region's best courses like New Yorkers do Shinnecock Hills Golf Club, Floridians do the Tournament Players Club Stadium Course, and North Carolinians do Pine-hurst No. 2.

As we said earlier, golfers in the metropolitan area have a lifetime's worth of dream courses. Unfortunately, they're also some of the most difficult courses to get on.

The next time you find yourself daydreaming about golf, try choosing courses within the metropolitan area that you'd dare dream to play—private or public.

Go ahead. I dare you. While you're at it, limit the selections to, say, a dozen.

A painful process. Try leaving off the list such dream private facilities as the historic Lower Course at Baltusrol, Tillinghast's Quaker Ridge, or a trio from seemingly endless Long Island gems like Deepdale, Garden City, and Meadow Brook. Omissions like those solidify an unparalleled wealth of golf courses in our metropolitan area.

New Yorkers reside in a golfer's dream world. Long Island alone has more than 100 facilities, and some are multi-course complexes.

But is there anywhere that is close to claiming property value on par with land that has Long Island foursome Shinnecock, National Golf Links, Maidstone, and Atlantic in its backyard? Just imagining a round on one of these creates goose bumps as if you're standing onsite while the sea air soaks into your skin.

It's the tradition of links, with ocean winds bending waist-high fescue to ground level and occasionally tormenting players with speckles of sand from dunes. It's the endless views from raised teeing areas, perfectly defined fairways, and contour-rich greens. It's the tradition that started with Shinnecock, considered to be the home of America's first 18-hole course and clubhouse. It's, it's. . .

"It's phenomenal land," reasons Rees Jones, the U.S. Open course doctor and lifelong metropolitan resident. "[Shinnecock] is a natural, coastal links-style golf course. It fits the land perfectly and has the old-style characteristics. . .You just have to position your shots. You're not home until you're home.

"Atlantic is a links-style golf course. There is not a bit of water on the course and it really looks like you're in the old country. National is the epitome of links design. [Its architect] Charles Blair Macdonald really brought the British ideas to America at the National Golf Links. You have to play it often to know how to play it. You have to play the bounces and know where to miss it and where not to miss it. Maidstone is probably the closest to a bona fide links of any course in America, because it sits right by the Atlantic Ocean. It's a very enjoyable golf course to play."

Maybe you've played one of our dozen fantasy designs or other dream courses in the metropolitan area. If you have, you've been treated to some of golf's most pristine opportunities.

Each round is forever entrenched in your mind. Whenever you want, you're allowed to return at no charge and without having to play in the shadow of a member. Just sit back and reminisce about that dream day.

Maybe you're awaiting your first close encounter of the special kind. In the meantime, continue to dream of where you'd be pleased beyond belief. That's what makes them dream courses.

1. Shinnecock Hills, Southhampton, NY: Corey Pavin's pinpoint shot took place at the home hole. Ray Floyd's lone under-par total to win the 1986 U.S. Open happened here. If you're a golf fan, Shinnecock Hills has a location for a panoramic view like no other: from the back of the Shinnecock clubhouse overlooking this magnificent course. Here's hoping many of you can open your eyes to that view in June of 2004 when the U.S. Open returns to Long Island for the second time in three years.

2. Maidstone Golf Club, East Hampton, NY: This is the elite of the elite, a one-of-a-kind creation of Willie Park Jr., winner of two British Opens (1887, 1889). This is a 6,403-yard test from the back tees that plays long enough even by today's standards. There are three cape holes, including the 17th, "one of the top five short par-4s in America," Jones says.

3. National Golf Links of America, Southhampton, NY: Shinnecock's neighbor is considered just as good if not better. Macdonald's masterpiece was known in the 1920s as a course ahead of its time and was mentioned in the same breath with St. Andrews. "It's got the best Redan hole in the world on the fourth hole," Jones says in reference to architects' concept born in North Berwick, Scotland, featuring a diagonal green that is sloped to the back and fronted by bunkers. "It's got some really fabulous (green) contours on the surfaces."

4. Bethpage Black, Farmingdale, NY: There isn't a "let-up" hole, from the opening dogleg right par-4 to the home green protected by cavernous bunkers. It is a Tillinghast design with a facelift from Jones. Country club conditions on a public course make it a joy to overcome somewhat difficult walking conditions. Enthusiastic U.S. Open crowds, strength of layout, and "muni course" image earned the course a return U.S. Open date for 2009. Under the stars at Beth-page—tonight's dream in the parking lot becomes tomorrow's reality.

5. Winged Foot Golf Club (West), Mamaroneck, NY: It has a world-signature clubhouse and a U.S. Open history almost second to none, like its champions: Bobby Jones (1929), Billy Casper (1959), Hale Irwin (1974), and Fuzzy Zoeller (1984). It must be doing something right, as the U.S. Open returns here in 2006. You have to go a ways to top Davis Love III's over-the-rainbow PGA Championship conquest in 1997. It's also the site for the 2004 U.S. Amateur.

6. Atlantic Golf Club, Bridgehampton, NY: This is a new-generation course among the Long Island elite private courses, but one that fits in. Let Jones talk about what makes his 1992 course a dream stop. "Sixth hole is one of the great short par-5s because it's got a fabulous green contour," he says. "The pocket in the middle can pull the ball off into another pocket. And, it's got four great short par-4s, which is hard for us to do."

7. Westchester Country Club (West), Rye, NY: One of my season-ending assignments for PGATOUR.COM in 2001 and 2002 was to ask rookies on the PGA Tour their favorite course. Some chose Westchester Country Club. They liked Walter Travis' design and the way it's presented for the Buick Classic. They liked the challenge of fairways weaving next to ankle-deep rough. And, they liked the venerable private hotel in the middle of the property. "Westchester was a lot of fun,"

recalled Ian Leggatt during his 2001 rookie campaign. "It's kind of an older, traditional-type place. It's a serious ball-strikers type course. You have to know where to hit it around the green and fit it around the golf course."

8. Stanwich Country Club, Greenwich, CT: Everyone once in their lives should experience course conditions as good as at Stanwich. Viewers of the nationally televised 2002 USGA Mid-Amateur saw only a glimpse of how good members have it at this exclusive facility. It's as if no grains of white sand are ever out of place. The course can be player-friendly until golfers try to solve Augusta National–like greens.

9. Essex County Country Club, West Orange, NJ: This is New Jersey's first country club. Thick tree-lined fairways are more spectacular when gazed backward from green to tee. Recently renovated, Essex County has some of the most spectacular fairway and greenside bunkering ever sprinkled on a golf course. They're breathtakingly defined and deep.

10. Ridgewood Country Club, Paramus, NJ: This is a tradition-rich, excellently manicured 27-hole course designed by Tillinghast. "A lot of diversity," Jones says, who reshaped the course's bunkers more than a dozen years ago. "It's got the real Tillinghast sculptured look. All three nines complement one another; they interchange and intermix. I always thought of Ridgewood as one of the prettiest golf courses in New Jersey." It presents a pleasant, old-style atmosphere that your grandparents would appreciate. It is beautifully tree-lined, but not too confining. One of its most memorable rounds came in 2001 when Arnold Palmer carded his age, a one-under-par 71, during the opening round of the Senior PGA Championship.

11. The Bridge, Bridgehampton, NY: Jones' Bridge course opened in 2002. Built on an old motor race track, the course takes golfers through nearly 7,400 yards where glaciers helped define the area. The views are so spectacular and

numerous that players will think every hole is within a snap-shot of the Peconic Bay or Sag Harbour. With about 60 members, the course is as exclusive as it gets. With a $500,000 fee to join, it's no wonder.

12. Trump National Golf Club, Briarcliff Manor, NY: Jim Fazio's design has some of the best driving holes around. Tee-ing areas are both picture-perfect and lethal. Playing the par-3 13th would always be memorable—how many holes do you play each year with an 80-foot waterfall behind the green? Trump National truly will be a dream facility following the completion of its clubhouse. Who wouldn't want to boast about being a member at The Donald's course?

the mental
game

Golf is a game. It's supposed to be relaxing and fun.

Who says golf is just a game? Tell that to the guy cursing moments after pelting his third consecutive ball out of bounds, turning a G-rated afternoon into an X-rated performance.

Who says golf is supposed to be relaxing? Tell that to the lady with her hands covering her face just after blasting the ball from one greenside bunker to another.

Who says golf is supposed to be fun? Tell that to the junior using the fairway as his personal runway to add air mileage to his pitching wedge. At that instant golf is not a game. Nor is it fun or relaxing.

Golf is a battle within. It's a mental game of trying not to let negative thoughts seep within the golf swing. Emotionally zapped professionals have the luxury of leaning on their personal mental gurus, the sports psychologists. Amateur players may not realize it, but they also have a mental guru, their local PGA professional.

Operators of driving ranges should purchase a couch for their professionals to use in hitting stalls. Instructors could take notes as players on the couch confess about ailing swing thoughts.

Detrimental images during pre-shot routines are major contributors to shanks, yips, skulls, and chunks. Not to be forgotten in the "Why–do–I–play?" list are duck hooks, slices, worm burners, pop-ups, and whiffs.

Positive images, on the other hand, produce birdie zones, crisp lob wedge connections off dirt-pan lies, and confident strokes down the stretch to seize $3 Nassaus. A new attitude is an open sesame to making golf relaxing, fun, and, most importantly, a game again.

"I do go to seminars, I've gone to (sports psychologist Dr. Bob) Rotella," says Tom Sutter, head professional at the Golf Club at Chelsea Piers. "I've gone to a visualization guy.

A lot of it is visualizing beforehand. An old pro told me when I was in college that I should have a picture of my round before I go to bed. So you go through the round the way you think it might be.

"But you can't write that in stone. It's not like when you get to the golf course and it's a shock when it doesn't happen. You get there and it's windy. . .You need a strong picture of what you'd like to have happen."

A reality check could make everyone's day more enjoyable, especially for single-digit players. These are talented amateurs who always opt to go for the green in two from a downhill lie, 240 yards from the green. Yet, they seem surprised when their shot caroms off one tree and into the woods, 30 yards shy of the green.

They should tie a string to their driver as a reminder on the first tee: Every player during every round will have both good and bad shots. Always.

Equal doses of confidence and reality intertwine to rescue emotionally spent golfers.

"It's not a game of perfect," says Ed Sorge, former long-time head professional at Silver Lake Golf Course. "There are times when you're going to have to recover. You need patience and concentration, and keep an even-keel attitude. Young people want to hit everything well, but it's not going to work that way."

Adds Sutter: "You can't really perform to your ability unless you're relaxed and confident."

An infinite number of downcast golfers use practice areas as their number one source for finding answers. They come here days before a tournament to correct what's bothering them. They come here immediately after poor rounds, attempting to make sure they'll have a good round tomorrow.

Driving ranges would be model locations for sports psychologists to set up shop. For now there isn't a sports psychologist's office at any of New York City's practice facilities, but you never know.

I stopped by Randalls Island Golf Center, home to one of two Manhattan driving ranges. Any sign of a sports psychologist? A worker was overseeing the snack bar and someone else was behind the counter to issue rental clubs.

In the back is Randalls Island's two-tier driving range. By the far right corner of the lower level someone is giving advice to a golfer.

Maybe a golf doctor is in.

Rick Nielsen isn't a sports psychologist. But to some Randalls Island regulars he might as well be considered their therapist. Nielsen has more than 20 years of teaching experience and is the head professional at Randalls Island.

While there wasn't a couch affixed to his private hitting booth, there was a nearby bench to sit on and vent about some of the biggest mental speed bumps that frequently slow a player's progress.

Problem: Some golfers lack confidence in tournaments.

Nielsen's cure: "There is golf and there is tournament golf. The best way to get better in tournament golf is to play in more tournaments. If it's your first or second tournament coming up, then you need to build a routine that you can count on. Play your own game. You can't be watching other players and trying to keep up with them because you're playing your own ball. Don't get down on yourself when you're out there. Try to have fun."

Problem: Finding a key swing thought before a tournament.

Nielsen's cure: "The day before an event I would work on my alignment. If it's way off I wouldn't touch it. I'd go to a balanced finish. I would work on maintaining tempo—that it's rhythmic, the same speed both ways. Easy things—picture feelings that you can bring to the golf course."

Problem: Finding a key swing thought during a tournament.

Nielsen's cure: "Try to stay positive and don't get down on yourself. If the ball goes into the trees, think of it as a challenge to try to make par rather than [looking at it] as a negative— 'Damn, I'm in the trees again. I stink.' The game of golf is how you deal with a dilemma. Somehow the world's best golfers hit in the trees and over greens and still make pars, where we feel like if we make a mistake that we're done for that hole."

Problem: Can you cure, dare we name the shot, the shank? Never can you hit just one shank.

Nielsen's cure: "What happens when you shank is 99 times out of a 100 you're coming down [too] steep. You're probably already aiming right and pulling left because the clubhead is coming across the ball with the hosel first. I would look at the inside quadrant of the golf ball. Maybe I'd step back a little bit from the golf ball. Try that."

Problem: First-tee jitters.

Nielsen cure: "The first swing needs to be a smooth motion. Don't try to hit the ball 300 yards off the first tee. Maybe take a 3-wood or a predictable club that you're comfortable with to get the ball in the fairway. That will automatically build confidence. If you're not in the fairway, you're playing defense."

Problem: Short putting woes often lead to numerous changes in putters.

Nielsen's cure: "What's happening is the golfer's mind is more on the clubface than on their hands. They need to get more in tune with their hands. If you watch their putts [you see that] as they get closer to the ball their hands stop and they push it. That can work into your chipping too because it's the same kind of motion. There are drills we do for that."

Problem: Some players take perfect practice swings. But when they hit the ball their swings are extremely different.

Nielsen's cure: "It's the same concept of the poor putter. Their mind is on the clubface. If you tell them to go over and swing at a leaf they would do it beautifully. If they swung at a tee it would be beautiful."

Problem: After you've been in a zone for three or four holes, how do you keep from becoming defensive?

Nielsen's cure: "I don't think of it that way. This year I shot a 67 on a course where it tied for the lowest (score) I've ever had. During the round I wasn't thinking that way. The ball just seemed to go in the hole more often than not. I didn't seem to hit it any better or putt it any better. I know that [defensive] thought, but you just try to go out and have fun and avoid thoughts like that. It will really screw you up."

Problem: Slumps may make players blame the ball, course superintendent, or players in his or her group. You may hear them complain, "The cups aren't cut right."

Nielsen's cure: "They're serious about it? If they're serious about it I don't know how to advise a person like that. That person is a negative thinker. No matter what, something is going to be wrong."

tournament play

If you're talking about the biggest amateur tournament in the five boroughs, it has to be the New York City Amateur.

The three-day event is traditionally held Memorial Day weekend at La Tourette Golf Course.

"It's the only major amateur event that brings everyone from all sorts of areas of New York City to play," says tournament director Steven Zuntag. "We have all the best players in the metropolitan area. We've also had people from all over the country."

Zuntag says he has as many as 500 entrants try to qualify at one of three courses in the boroughs. Players must have a minimum index of 8.0 to sign up. Minimum handicaps for seniors (50–59) and super seniors (60 and over) are higher.

Wall Street trader Mike Stamberger easily won in 2003 and was the only player to finish under par. "[La Tourette] gives up their opening week of their golf season for the tournament. That should tell you how much they like the tournament," says Stamberger, who finished with a three-day total of 213 (three under par). New York City golfers who call one of 13 city facilities their home course can play in Metropolitan Golf Association (MGA) events. They simply have to be a member of their course's golf organization and have a handicap card.

Men interested in playing in the MGA Public Links championship must have a handicap index of 8.0 or less. Women are required to have a 20.0 or less to be eligible for the Women's Public Links event. Higher handicap players can consider signing up for the Net Team championship.

For more information about MGA events, call 914-347-4653.

Maybe you're more interested playing in a tournament on your home course, from serious to friendly competitions. Check the calendar's list of events in the pro shop.

Dyker Beach Golf Course has annual tournaments on Memorial Day and Labor Day. Every May, the course plays host to a Women's Golf Day to introduce new women players to the game. Proceeds go to Breast Cancer Awareness. Every summer, the Brooklyn course usually entertains four nine-hole "night golf" tournaments.

Tournament golf isn't unfamiliar to golf-crazed New York City fans. But it's as much about them watching big-time golf as playing it.

This summer, city golf fans won't have to travel too far to attend both the U.S. Open (Shinnecock Hills) and the U.S. Amateur (Winged Foot, West Course). The following year the PGA Championship will be played at Baltusrol's Lower Course for the first time. Winged Foot West will be home to the 2006 U.S. Open. And, in 2009 the Black Course at Bethpage State Park will play host to its second U.S. Open in seven years.

The PGA Tour, Champions Tour, and LPGA also continue to make regular-season stops in the metropolitan area.

golf lingo

Welcome to Golf Terminology 101 with 18 catch phrases. While there won't be a test afterward, take note that many relate to New York City players.

In the leather: A putt that is shorter than the distance from the bottom of the putter to the grip. Does anyone use leather grips anymore? And does the rule include those extra-long belly putters? I bet the boys in the Sandtrappers Club at Dyker Beach have it in their by-laws that it's an automatic disqualification from their club if you use one of those fancy-schmancy belly putters.

Out of bounds: If from Clearview Golf Course you hit a shot onto the Clearview Expressway, it's safe to say you're out of bounds.

Home-course advantage: If you're playing Kissena Park Golf Course and its many elevation changes for the first time, it's wise not to involve yourself in a money game with one of the course regulars. There is home-course advantage and there is the Kissena Park home-course advantage.

Practice makes perfect: That's all you can do when it comes to playing golf in Manhattan.

Press: It means to add a bet to the original bet. Wonder how many times "press" has been used on the city courses by some of New York City's major moneybags?

Forecaddies: They traditionally accompany groups to speed up play. Their services, meanwhile, would never help city pace-of-play issues.

Bump and run: This shot is traditionally used from 20 to 30 yards from the green with the ball barely soaring above the ground. But city players may have used it from 120 to 130 yards before the new irrigation systems were installed.

Dogleg right: It's a hole design that veers right. Right? Maybe. Princess the dog makes Dyker Beach fairways her home turf. So if you're on the Brooklyn course and Princess is within view to your right, well, it's a dogleg right. In fact, it's four dog legs right.

Hole-in-one: While it's always a big deal if you score an ace, there are penalties to be paid afterward. Say, the hefty bar tab with your name next to "drinks on me." City courses are normally packed and so are their bars. If you get an ace in the city, don't tell anyone until the next day.

Flop shot: It takes extraordinary nerves to consistently pull off this lofty pitch shot from a smooth lie in the fairway. But if someone demonstrates a deft lob-wedge touch off a dirt-pan lie, don't wage even a dime against him or her.

Golf historian: Many old hands qualify for this honorary distinction from their favorite city course. These are the ones who should claim their golf course as their home address on their W2s.

Rare iron: Ask your father if he remembers the 1-iron. Now nearly obsolete, the 1-iron was replaced by utility metal woods or a specialty wedge.

Winter rules in the metropolitan area: If you play in the city, you'll be on a course unless a blanket of snow gets there first. Play outside the city and you're left dreaming of the next time you can play, likely in March or April.

The wrist waggle: You used to see this move a lot in pre-shot routines. Maybe PGA Tour player Sergio Garcia made it a crime.

Big hitters: Where were all the big hitters before superduper golf balls and metal and titanium-faced drivers? Now, it's as if every foursome has at least one "big hitter."

Fore!: A four-letter word not used enough.

Not for members only: Men and women can join clubs at various city courses without high dues.

The serious New York City golfer: The one who plays the 13 city courses in one season.

index